Joe Pisapia, LLC

Presents

THE FANTASY BASEBALL BLACK BOOK

2025 Edition

Joe Pisapia @JoePisapia17

Christopher Welsh @IsItTheWelsh

Kelly Kirby @thewonkypenguin

Brian Entrekin @bdentrek

Joe Orrico @JoeOrrico99

Edited by: Kelly Kirby

Cover Art by Ethan Woodward

Follow us: Facebook: Fantasy Black Book Instagram @fantasyblackbook

©2025 Fantasy Black Book Sports; Joe Pisapia, LLC

FantasyPros
Fantasy Baseball Podcast

Available everywhere you listen to podcasts

&

FantasyPros MLB YouTube Leading Off LIVE

Mon-Fri on the FantasyPros MLB YouTube Channel

Subscribe today!

2025 RPV DRAFT CHEAT SHEETS NOW AVAILABLE

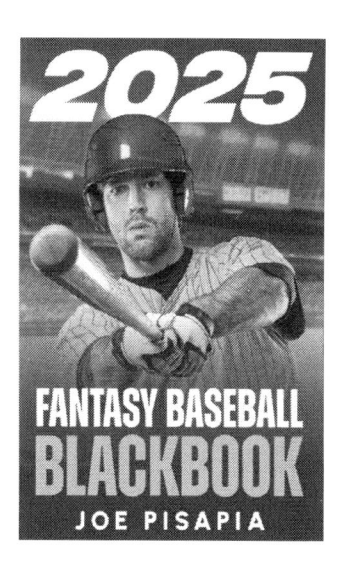

If you want the most up to date RPV on one easy to reference PDF cheat sheet for your drafts

Send $5 to:

PayPal: fantasyblackbook@gmail.com

or Venmo: @FantasyBlackBook

Subject: "Cheat Sheets" & enclose your return email address.

One time cost, with FREE automatic updates sent in Feb & March!

GET YOURS TODAY!

About the Authors:

Joe Pisapia is the author of the #1 best-selling Fantasy Black Book Series, and creator of the revolutionary player evaluation tool, Relative Position Value (RPV). He currently hosts The FantasyPros Baseball and Football Podcasts, as well as The BettingPros NFL Podcast. Joe is also a TV host at SportsGrid and can be seen on Fantasy Sports Today Sundays 8-10 am est and on SXM.

Christopher Welsh (aka "The Welsh") is a 10-year fantasy sports analyst working for FantasyPros as a host and analyst on the baseball flagship show, "Leading Off." Welsh co-created the In This League fantasy podcasts, as well as Prospect One, the fantasy prospect podcast. Welsh has been a featured regular analyst on CBS Sports Fantasy Baseball today podcast and The Athletic's Rates and Barrels. Welsh did not pitch for Cincinnati Reds in the 70's, nor is he John Lackey. Iconic twitter handle @isitthwelsh.

Kelly Kirby is a content specialist at FantasyPros and BettingPros and works with all things fantasy baseball, including article writing, editing, and podcasting. Perhaps better known as The Wonkypenguin, she also views herself as the Patron Saint of Underrepresented Sports, creating and updating player prop models for the NHL and WNBA on a daily basis during those seasons. However, fantasy baseball is her first love, and she almost won a 2024 league because of Victor Robles, which would have been her proudest accomplishment to date. Kelly enjoys doling out advice all season long and diving into research first thing in the offseason. She lives in Minnesota with all the dogs she's legally allowed.

Brian Entrekin (aka KC Bubba) has been podcasting and writing about Fantasy Baseball for nine years. This will be my fifth year contributing to the Fantasy Black Book, and I could not be more excited. I am the host of the Benched with Bubba Podcast, co-host of Bubba & the Bloom, as well as many more podcasts. I currently run my own Substack (KC Bubba's Substack) and you can find my other written work at Baseball HQ and Fantasy Pros. Lastly, I am always available on Twitter (@bdentrek) if you ever have any questions.

Joe Orrico is a writer and podcast host/producer for FanGraphs and FantasyPros. He has a background in journalism and sports media and has been producing fantasy sports content since 2021. You can hear him on his solo podcast, "90 Feet From Home Fantasy Baseball" throughout the season as well as periodically on the FantasyPros Baseball Podcast and The Sleeper and the Bust Podcast. You can find him on the various social media platforms @JoeOrrico99

Table of Contents

Introduction

Chapter 1: Relative Position Value

Chapter 2: Draft Strategies

Chapter 3: Starting Pitchers

Chapter 4: Relief Pitchers

Chapter 5: Catchers

Chapter 6: First Basemen

Chapter 7: Second Basemen

Chapter 8: Third Basemen

Chapter 9: Shortstops

Chapter 10: Outfielders

Chapter 11: 2025 Prospects

Chapter 1

RELATIVE POSITION VALUE (RPV)

Joe Pisapia

Whether you play in roto formats or points leagues, the key to success is value. It's always about value! Premium players at premium prices should deliver premium productivity. When they don't, you have teams that struggle. When you hit on players at lower draft costs that outperform their ADP, you have teams that succeed. Besides player talent, so much of a player's value is tied to their position. Even more importantly, a player's value is tied to the depth of that position that the league you're playing in utilizes. Many value-based drafting systems get this wrong, and the player pool shifts annually, making different positions more/less valuable.

Relative Position Value (RPV) exists to clarify player value in fantasy. There will be your very standard roto leagues, but there will also be leagues you play in with strange scoring wrinkles and odd lineup requirements. RPV will help you in all of these scenarios. RPV is simple and applicable. In the world of fantasy sports, you will see rankings, rankings, and more rankings. Some places will at least give your tiers within those rankings. RPV gives you quantified rankings and visual tiers. You will be able to see where the drop-off is in cold, hard numbers. RPV will also illustrate players who have negative effects on your roster. The types of players that can bring down your team's productivity, especially if you overpay for them. You will also see how dramatic the drop-offs are and how positions as a whole look in terms of strength and weakness.

RPV in the Black Book considers projections, previous season statistics, and 3-year averages (when applicable) to create a more sophisticated perspective of a player's worth. Projections can be helpful but not relied upon solely. When was the last time projectionists were held accountable (or held themselves accountable) for their failures? The answer is hardly ever. Projections can have their place when you couple them with reality. RPV is so useful because it can be adapted for every league's depth. A 10-team league approach differs greatly from a 12 or 14-team league because the player pool's depth changes the value's perspective. RPV is more than a system; it's an actual strategy. Fantasy coverage is full of great stats, information, and well-informed opinions. What it's annually lacking is applying that to a strategy. That's where the Black Book will separate you from the pack. This is your edge over your competition.

RPV IN PRACTICE

The Fantasy Black Book formula is more complicated than the "basic" version I will present to you. At the core, the way to determine the RPV -- or the percentage in which a player is better than the fantasy league average -- is:

(Individual Player Point Value – Fantasy League Average of the Position) ÷ Fantasy League Average of the Position = RPV

So, what is the "Fantasy League Average"? Every league has a different number of teams and a varying number of active players at a given position. Some have five active outfielders, some CINF/MINF slots, others play multiple UT slots, and so on.

The Fantasy League Average is whatever the average production is from a position based on your league's depth. For example, if your league has 12 managers and starts one 2B every week and a MINF slot, the 2B pool will probably push into the 24 range based on players with multiple eligibility and bats you'd want on your fantasy team. If the top player at 2B scored 600 points and the 24th scored around 300, the fantasy league average is likely somewhere around 450 points. All players who score above this mark are "Positive RPV" players. The ones below are "Negative RPV" players.

Fantasy sports is a simple game of out-scoring your opponents as frequently as possible from as many active positions as possible. The more your team lives in the "Positive," the greater your chances are week-to-week. It's like playing the odds in Texas Hold'em. The odds are in your favor if you have a strong starting hand. Sure, you may take some bad beats, but more often than not, the percentages will play in your favor.

Here's a look at first base using the final stats of last season and the RPV formula to show you how they finished in actual RPV. You will see the depth for a 12-team league that uses corner infield spots in a starting lineup (16 is a good number accounting for players that qualify at other positions, takes into account some CINF spots will be taken up by third basemen and some first basemen will be used as utility bats). You will also see a deeper league RPV that covers 14 teams or more.

	Leagues w/o CINF	Proj FPTS	RPV
1	Vladimir Guerrero 1B,3B | TOR	598	29%
2	Anthony Santander 1B,OF | BAL	545.5	18%
3	Bryce Harper 1B | PHI	520	12%
4	Freddie Freeman 1B | LAD	505	9%
5	Josh Naylor 1B | CLE	496.5	7%
6	Pete Alonso 1B | NYM	482	4%
7	Spencer Steer 1B,2B,3B,OF | CIN	474	2%
8	Matt Olson 1B | ATL	470	1%
9	Salvador Perez 1B,C | KC	442.5	-5%
10	Alec Bohm 1B,3B | PHI	428	-8%
11	Alec Burleson 1B,OF | STL	413	-11%
12	Jake Cronenworth 1B,2B | SD	413	-11%
13	Brendan Donovan 1B,2B,OF | STL	411	-11%
14	Luis Arraez 1B,2B | SD	409	-12%
15	Vinnie Pasquantino 1B | KC	407.5	-12%
16	Cody Bellinger 1B,OF | CHC	405.5	-13%

	Leagues w/ CINF	Proj FPTS	RPV
1	Vladimir Guerrero 1B,3B | TOR	598	36%
2	Anthony Santander 1B,OF | BAL	545.5	24%
3	Bryce Harper 1B | PHI	520	19%
4	Freddie Freeman 1B | LAD	505	15%
5	Josh Naylor 1B | CLE	496.5	13%
6	Pete Alonso 1B | NYM	482	10%
7	Spencer Steer 1B,2B,3B,OF | CIN	474	8%
8	Matt Olson 1B | ATL	470	7%
9	Salvador Perez 1B,C | KC	442.5	1%
10	Alec Bohm 1B,3B | PHI	428	-2%
11	Alec Burleson 1B,OF | STL	413	-6%
12	Jake Cronenworth 1B,2B | SD	413	-6%
13	Brendan Donovan 1B,2B,OF | STL	411	-6%
14	Luis Arraez 1B,2B | SD	409	-7%
15	Vinnie Pasquantino 1B | KC	407.5	-7%
16	Cody Bellinger 1B,OF | CHC	405.5	-8%
17	Yainer Diaz 1B,C | HOU	402.5	-8%
18	Christian Walker 1B | ARI	402.5	-8%
19	Isaac Paredes 1B,2B,3B | CHC	401	-9%
20	Carlos Santana 1B | MIN	399.5	-9%
21	Paul Goldschmidt 1B | STL	387.5	-12%
22	Jake Burger 1B,3B | MIA	376.5	-14%
23	Yandy Diaz 1B | TB	369.5	-16%
24	Michael Busch 1B,3B | CHC	362.5	-17%

The RPV shows us that Vlad Guerrero dominated; Santander and Harper were definitive advantages; Freddie Freeman, Matt Olson, and Pete Alonso didn't return their draft stock; and Josh Naylor was a huge win in return on investment. In deeper leagues, there wasn't much of a "soft middle" in terms of fantasy league average at the position. Only eight of the 24 first basemen were in the positive. That's probably why you felt some of your teams struggled with weak corner infield options. This information can become an advantage in 2025 drafts by recognizing how the tiers drop off, when to draft a player, and when to pass because they will not move the needle.

As fantasy players, we know inherently where we succeeded and failed in a draft, but RPV can show you in black and white how to define those wins and losses. RPV can also lead you on the path to success when using the system to avoid these losses and take advantage of player values that can outperform their ADP, one of the keys to winning leagues.

So, how do we use RPV to create "core roster strength" and dominate your league mates from as many roster spots as you can on a daily, weekly, monthly, or even season-long basis?

RPV IN THEORY

"SP isn't a position, BUT SP1 is!"

With so many different formats of fantasy baseball, a player's value can vary a great deal. Most mixed roto leagues start with nine SP slots. Most managers will have a #1 starter on their roster. In H2H formats (points and categories), pitching values can vastly vary depending on the scoring or weight of each stat. The trick is to understand how to exploit SP, or any position for that matter, by building roster strength.

Last year, Tarik Skubal scored 612 fantasy points as the #1 overall SP. The fifth pitcher in points leagues was Cole Ragans at 490 pts. The 12th guy was Jack Flaherty at 451 pts. So, how much more valuable is each one of these guys compared to the other? Before we get ahead of ourselves, let's first see the formula in action. The Fantasy League Average (FLA) of the top 16 SP1s is 486 pts (down from 505 last year).

Here's the trick! Every team will likely have **one genuine SP1 or OF1**, meaning SP1/OF1 are unique scoring positions. Rather than create a fantasy league average for 24 overall, it's more applicable to separate them into private groups and create an individual fantasy league average for each.

Now that we understand Fantasy League Average, let's get more specific. We'll use 16 as a base size group because in your 12-team league with nine pitcher spots, typically, seven are SP and two are RP (with variance, of course). But 12 teams times seven pitchers equals 84, and 84 divided by 5 (as in a 5-man rotation) is roughly 16.

Tarik Skubal scored 612 pts, and the Fantasy League Average was 486. Subtract that Fantasy League Average from Skubal's 612, then divide by that same FLA (486 pts), and you have a **Relative Position Value of +10.2% RPV**: [612-486] ÷ 486 = 25.9%. That means Strider was 26% more productive than the average SP1 last year. That is a quantifiable value and an understanding of Strider's value as an SP1 compared to his peers in the top tier.

2024 FINAL SP RPV for SP1 (Top 16):

	Player	FPTS	RPV
1	Tarik Skubal SP | DET	612	26%
2	Chris Sale SP | ATL	589	21%
3	Zack Wheeler SP | PHI	576	19%
4	Dylan Cease SP | SD	514	6%
5	Cole Ragans RP,SP | KC	490	1%
6	Logan Gilbert SP | SEA	484	0%
7	Aaron Nola SP | PHI	473	-3%
8	Shota Imanaga SP | CHC	470	-3%
9	Seth Lugo SP | KC	466	-4%
10	Corbin Burnes SP | BAL	454	-7%
11	Jack Flaherty SP | LAD	451	-7%
12	Pablo Lopez SP | MIN	451	-7%
13	George Kirby SP | SEA	439	-10%
14	Sonny Gray SP | STL	438	-10%
15	Carlos Rodon SP | NYY	437	-10%
16	Paul Skenes SP | PIT	433	-11%

2024 FINAL SP RPV for SP2

	Player	FPTS	RPV
17	Michael King RP,SP | SD	429	8%
18	Bailey Ober SP | MIN	429	8%
19	Framber Valdez SP | HOU	420	6%
20	Ronel Blanco RP,SP | HOU	413	4%
21	Logan Webb SP | SF	409	3%
22	Bryce Miller SP | SEA	400	1%
23	Tanner Bibee SP | CLE	395	-1%
24	Garrett Crochet RP,SP | CHW	394	-1%
25	Yusei Kikuchi SP | HOU	391	-2%
26	Hunter Brown SP | HOU	388	-2%
27	Sean Manaea RP,SP | NYM	388	-2%
28	Jose Berrios SP | TOR	385	-3%
29	Kevin Gausman SP | TOR	380	-4%
30	Max Fried SP | ATL	380	-4%
31	Freddy Peralta SP | MIL	377	-5%
32	Luis Castillo SP | SEA	374	-6%

Due to injuries to guys like Spencer Strider and the fall off of some stalwart veterans, SP1 was extremely top-heavy last year. However, if you went with last year's Black Book approach and drafted in bulk, targeting guys like Seth Lugo and Shota Imanaga, whom I was extremely high on last year, then you were likely a very competitive team. SP2, on the other hand, is a clump. A nice, productive, relatively safe clump, but a clump nonetheless. The RPV shows why environment matters so much for guys like Garrett Crochet, who pitch on bad teams. It illuminates how far Kevin Gausman fell from a top 5 guy in 2023 to a low-level SP2. The lesson here for a second straight year is to buy quality in quantity over premium starters at premium prices. The fantasy league average SP1 dropped from 505 to 486 points, signaling starting pitchers continue to impact games less every year from a fantasy productivity standpoint. Therefore, you can be far more competitive with a solid rotation than with a "stars and scrubs/streamers" approach.

So, how can the fantasy player exploit RPV?

By having a high-end SP1 and then drafting ANOTHER SP1 as your SP2, you have "frontloaded" the position and created an area of strength.

The BIGGEST mistake fantasy owners make in any sport is "filling their roster for positions" instead of filling their roster with talent and strength. This same approach can be exploited with outfielders, especially in five active OF league setups like most roto. Starting with Acuna is excellent! Following up with another high-end OF is even better. You create an RPV advantage and weaken the player pool at that position simultaneously. You also make roster strength!

When you fill your roster for positions, you get a mediocre .500 team. When you fill your roster with core strength somewhere, you have an advantage over the rest of the field. That roster strength can carry your season as long as you can responsibly fill the other positions and avoid negative RPV as often as possible.

With MLB teams limiting so many young arms, the real aces are worth more than ever in H2H formats, especially points leagues. By "frontloading" elite SP, you can dominate. By frontloading OF in a five-active league, you can dominate. RPV is the ultimate tool to truly define talent and, even more importantly, where the drop-off in talent lies. Rankings are biased. RPV is honest.

So, why does frontloading a position work?

Well, as an SP1, Aaron Nola had a -3% RPV advantage. If you drafted, say, Zach Wheeler as your #1 and Nola as your #2, Nola's RPV as an SP2 would have soared to +19% RPV advantage in that class. The advantage continues as you draft an SP2 as a #3 and so on. The same can be said for OF or 1B or any position. Don't just take players for a roster spot. Take the best players to create a strong roster. Targeting guys who can potentially jump a tier is also essential. Every year, we talk about a player being "a steal" or a league winner. RPV quantifies this feeling with cold, hard numbers.

NOTE: AN SP1 OR AN OF1 IS ALWAYS A BETTER SELECTION THAN AN SP2 OR OF2 ETC. RPV IS CREATED BASED ON COMPARING GROUPS OF PLAYERS AT POSITIONS TO THEMSELVES IN TIERS, AND A TIER 1 PLAYER IS RANKED IN THAT TIER FOR A REASON. DESPITE LOW-END TIER 1 GUYS HAVING NEGATIVE RPV, THEY'D BE TOP OF THE BOARD/POSITIVE RPV IF THEY WERE IN TIER 2.

Now that we've outlined RPV, let's dive deeper.

RPV IN-SEASON

RPV IN PRACTICE (Draft and Trades)

Now more than ever, no "one ranking system" will be useful to you in any format. Ignore these Top 100 lists and nonsense like that – and instead, focus on the player's actual value and weight in your league. That's why RPV works. With so many fantasy baseball styles, it's crucial to understand the value of each position in your league. RPV will help you assess talent to hit season-long 5x5 category thresholds and just as easily dominate H2H and play DFS.

The last best thing about RPV is that it strips away a lot of the hype and noise surrounding the athletes and fictional computer projections that can be misleading and downright destructive.

RPV is about understanding a player's value -- his ACTUAL value. Not what his value may be projected to be while you sit in last place, wondering where you went wrong. The best way to evaluate a player is through a mixture of career averages, previous statistics, and projections that are then weighed against the other players of the same position. NOT PROJECTIONS ALONE!

Using only last year's numbers will give you a great team ... for last season. Using just projections will provide you with a great team ... in theory. RPV will deliver you a great team in REALITY!

You can choose to be great at one spot or two, but if you are below average at other places, your overall RPV will even out. You may find yourself managing a middle-of-the-road team. Being above-average in as many places as possible, even without a top-flight star, you will consistently out-produce your opponents. If you use RPV correctly, you may even find yourself above average in most places and great in others, making you the one to beat. It's the ability to adapt, adjust, and understand that separates us. RPV is the difference-maker.

RPV can not only tell you how much better a player is than the average for his position but also how much better he is than the next guy available at his position on the draft board. Understanding these RPV relationships is a key technique in maximizing your positional advantage.

To illustrate this point and its application, let's take a draft day example. It's your pick, and you have openings to fill at 2B and SS. The top available players on the board at each position look like this:

2B

- Player A: +25% RPV
- Player B: +20% RPV
- Player C: +18% RPV
- Player D: +16% RPV
- Player E: +15% RPV

SS

- Player F: +18% RPV
- Player G: +4% RPV
- Player H: +2% RPV
- Player I: 0% RPV
- Player J: -4% RPV

At first glance, you might be inclined to take Player A, who is 25% better than the average at his position. All other things being equal, Player F is the better choice. Even though he is only 18% better than the average, the drop-off between him and the next-best player at his position is 14 percentage points. That's a significant drop-off. If you take Player A now, Player F almost definitely won't be on the board when your next pick rolls around, and at best, you'll be stuck with a very average guy (Player I is the average SS in your league at 0%RPV), or below average shortstop.

However, if you take Player F now, you'll be on the right side of that 14% RPV advantage over the teams who haven't drafted a 2B yet. You'll also probably lose out on Player A at 2B, but you will still most likely get someone from the above list (Player C, D, or E), all of whom are trading in the same RPV range. You have only lost eight percentage points. It may not sound like a lot, but it is, and it adds up the more you fall below or rise above the middle line. By picking this way, you end up with a decisive advantage at one position and still above average at the other. The alternative is being above average at one position and decidedly average or worse at the other, which is why many fantasy owners fail. And usually, they base these decisions on the name of the player instead of their RPV.

The owner who does that effectively has a distinct advantage. Remember, don't marginalize your strength for the sake of filling a position. Create roster strength instead!

FAQs

How does RPV help me in Roto?
Value is value. Yes, to a certain extent you need to hit benchmarks in terms of categories. However, RPV will show you how to approach players who contribute to those benchmarks. Not overpaying for players that only impact one or two categories positively, or worse players that help in some and hurt in others, all of that is there in RPV drafting strategy.

Do you do a Top 100 List?
No. They are a fun but futile exercise. Drafts are like snowflakes. They are all unique. Being prepared and flexible is what's important. It's important to draft the right players at the right value. Lists are just opinions. Informed ones, but opinions. They are NOT a strategy.

But what about my weird league scoring?
You can use RPV independently in circumstances where league scoring is very strange. Just drop in the formula and use the host site projections. It won't be as good as what I give you in the Black Book, but it will at least be a working RPV you can use in your more peculiar league-scoring situations.

Chapter 2

Draft Strategies

Roto Draft Strategy

By KC Bubba

4-Round Draft Strategy

	ROUND 1	ROUND 2	ROUND 3	ROUND 4
Team 1	Shohei Ohtani	Austin Riley	William Contreras	Pablo Lopez
Team 2	Bobby Witt Jr.	Rafael Devers	George Kirby	Felix Bautista
Team 3	Aaron Judge	Jackson Merrill	Matt Olson	Yainer Diaz
Team 4	Elly De La Cruz	Jazz Chisholm Jr.	Emmanuel Clase	Jose Altuve
Team 5	Jose Ramirez	Ketel Marte	Chris Sale	Mason Miller
Team 6	Gunnar Henderson	Logan Gilbert	Manny Machado	Gerri Cole
Team 7	Kyle Tucker	Freddie Freeman	Oneil Cruz	Yoshinobu Yamamoto
Team 8	Corbin Carroll	Trea Turner	Jacob deGrom	Wyatt Langford
Team 9	Juan Soto	Bryce Harper	Corbin Burnes	Devin Williams
Team 10	Julio Rodriguez	Jaren Duran	Corey Seager	Dylan Cease
Team 11	Mookie Betts	Zack Wheeler	Garrett Crochet	Ozzie Albies
Team 12	Fernando Tatis Jr.	Ronald Acuna	CJ Abrams	James Wood
Team 13	Paul Skenes	Jackson Chourio	Michael Harris II	Edwin Diaz
Team 14	Tarik Skubal	Vladimir Guerrero Jr.	Blake Snell	Josh Hader
Team 15	Francisco Lindor	Yordan Alvarez	Pete Alonso	Cole Ragans

Roto Strategy Overview

As we enter 2025, there are a lot of excellent 5-category hitters to target early in drafts. Shohei Ohtani, Bobby Witt Jr., and Aaron Judge are the consensus Top 3 picks, with Elly De La Cruz working his way into the conversation for some. Pitching is also solid, with the two young guns of Paul Skenes and Tarik Skubal sneaking into the first round. With the depth of hitters, you can wait on pitching till Round 3 or 4 unless you want one of Skenes or Skubal.

I prefer to get at least three hitters early to help with the batting average, as that statistic starts drying up quickly throughout the draft. You can find power and speed as the draft goes on. The reason to take at least one pitcher early is for ratios, but more importantly, for elite strikeout skills. Only a handful of pitchers can get 200+ strikeouts, and those pitchers go in the early rounds. Closers are going early as the elite closers have separated themselves from the field in recent years, but you can wait on closers if you feel comfortable in the later rounds and the waiver wire.

Season Long vs. H2H Roto

There are always some differentials when looking at season-long versus H2H leagues. For hitters, you want that week-to-week consistency more than the volatility you can deal with in season-long leagues. Elly De La Cruz is a great example of a player who can be more volatile as he can be incredibly streaky, whereas Jose Ramirez is as consistent as they come and gains more appeal in H2H.

Pitchers should also get more love as the aces will give you much more consistency for H2H leagues, where waiting on pitchers can leave you much more volatile to lose in the pitching categories from week to week. This is also true for relief pitchers, as you need those weekly saves and better ratios that the elite closers provide. You should be more aggressive to win that week-to-week saves category. If you don't care about saves, you can almost punt the position, stacking up stats elsewhere.

Mock Draft Review

Looking at the early rounds, I love taking hitters in the first two rounds and then grabbing an ace like Garrett Crochet or another in that pocket. In Round 4, I will usually go back to another bat and wait on closers, but that becomes a personal decision at that point. You should target at least one outfielder, if not two, in the first few rounds as the top tier of the position begins to deteriorate. The same can be said for shortstops. There are plenty of mid-tier starting pitchers, and as the draft goes on, the need to double-tap starting pitching early is less strongly needed than in previous seasons. The moral of the story is to get an ace and load up on five-category bats, focusing on an elite batting average.

Points League Draft Strategy

By Joe Pisapia

4-Round Draft Strategy

	ROUND 1	ROUND 2	ROUND 3	ROUND 4
Team 1	Shohei Ohtani	Manny Machado	Corbin Burnes	Blake Snell
Team 2	Bobby Witt Jr.	Rafael Devers	Logan Gilbert	Anthony Santander
Team 3	Aaron Judge	Trea Turner	Dylan Cease	George Kirby
Team 4	Jose Ramirez	Paul Skenes	Jarren Duran	Framber Valdez
Team 5	Gunnar Henderson	Zack Wheeler	Gerrit Cole	Marcell Ozuna
Team 6	Juan Soto	Freddie Freeman	Chris Sale	Pablo Lopez
Team 7	Mookie Betts	Bryce Harper	Aaron Nola	Pete Alonso
Team 8	Elly De La Cruz	Julio Rodriguez	Willy Adames	Logan Webb
Team 9	Ronald Acuna Jr.	Corbin Carroll	Jackson Merrill	Corey Seager
Team 10	Francisco Lindor	Yordan Alvarez	Bryce Miller	Jose Altuve
Team 11	Vladimir Guerrero Jr.	Kyle Tucker	Jackson Chourio	Zac Gallen
Team 12	Tarik Skubal	Fernando Tatis Jr.	Ketel Marte	Cole Ragans

Points League Overview

Once upon a time, points league drafts had a 50% starting pitcher ratio in the first round. Those days are gone. I'm content to grab an ace at value in the first few rounds, but equally pleased to draft offense early and often and then build a deep quality rotation. Even though I may not have that one dominant starter, ask the managers who drafted Gerrit Cole and Spencer Strider last year. Sure, injuries can happen to anyone at any time. However, it's foolish to put our heads in the sand and think that anyone nowadays is as dominant as the days of Randy Johnson and Pedro Martinez of yesteryear or, frankly, even the Roy Halladay, Clayton Kershaw, Justin Verlander, Max Scherzer types from just 10 years ago. Those pitchers all were influencing 230 or more innings annually. Just four pitchers crossed 200 innings in '24. Ten years ago, that number was 34. Simply put, the fewer innings you garner, the less opportunity you have to rack up fantasy points, whether it be strikeouts, wins, quality starts, etc. Give me the strong all-around offensive players, and I will find my pitching value and buy in bulk Costco style.

Mock Draft Review

The earliest I would take a pitcher this year is probably Pick 10. Tarik Skubal could go anywhere from Pick 3 to the Pick 12 turn, but to maximize the draft board value and the risk/limitations of pitching in 2025, the later, the better. Pitching hits its peak value late Round 2-Round 3, although I personally prefer to do offense rounds 1-2 and then hit pitching in bulk over the next few rounds. Team 6 is a great example of smashing value and balance simultaneously. Most teams will want to grab at least one starter in the first four rounds, possibly two. That means if you have a very clear ranking of your value arms from SP No. 20 on, then you could, in theory, draft four straight hitters and then go SP the next three rounds, ending up with a rotation of, say, Michael King, Sonny Gray, and Tanner Bibee. That is also a very viable approach, building a team on offense and then a rotation with high-end depth.

Dynasty Strategy

By KC Bubba

4-Round Draft Strategy

	ROUND 1	ROUND 2	ROUND 3	ROUND 4
Team 1	Bobby Witt Jr.	Jackson Holliday	Bo Bichette	Royce Lewis
Team 2	Shohei Ohtani	Spencer Strider	Adley Rutschman	Triston Casas
Team 3	Ronald Acuna Jr.	Luis Robert Jr.	Logan Gilbert	Gerrit Cole
Team 4	Julio Rodriguez	Michael Harris II	Corbin Burnes	Masyn Winn
Team 5	Juan Soto	Pete Alonso	Francisco Lindor	Shota Imanaga
Team 6	Kyle Tucker	Corey Seager	Wyatt Langford	Zach Neto
Team 7	Fernando Tatis Jr.	Ozzie Albies	George Kirby	Travis Bazzana
Team 8	Corbin Carroll	Trea Turner	Junior Caminero	Andrew Painter
Team 9	Jackson Chourio	Bryce Harper	William Contreras	Jackson Jobe
Team 10	Vladimir Guerrero Jr.	Tarik Skubal	Jasson Dominguez	Jarren Duran
Team 11	Aaron Judge	Paul Skenes	Yoshinobu Yamamoto	Seiya Suzuki
Team 12	Gunnar Henderson	Austin Riley	James Wood	Blake Snell
Team 13	Elly De La Cruz	Mat Olson	Dylan Crews	Matt McLain
Team 14	Jose Ramirez	Freddie Freeman	Jackson Merrill	Oneil Cruz
Team 15	Yordan Alvarez	Rafael Devers	CJ Abrams	Manny Machado

Dynasty Strategy Overview

We are living in a golden age of elite young talent. There have been bats for days with young arms, and Paul Skenes and Tarik Skubal have showcased their skills this past season. There are two ways to go about building your team. Play to win now, or play for the future. There are many 25-30-year-old talents that you can draft early and immediately contend. There are also a ton of prospects or players that have played a year or two, so build your team around a long-term plan.

I prefer to win now, so I would draft young studs like Bobby Witt Jr. and surround him with plenty of other core hitters. I am always interested in waiting on pitching in dynasty, as their injuries seem more frequent and profound. You can always draft or trade for pitching later if you load up on elite hitters.

Mock Draft Review

As you can see in the draft, there is an emphasis on hitters early, but there are still plenty of starting pitchers if you see fit. The beauty of a dynasty draft is that the picks can look so different from draft to draft, depending on the strategy in play. There are fourth-rounders above that some may take much earlier, changing the whole draft.

Another tweak, compared to season-long drafts, is the need to build quality and not worry as much to double up on positions or avoid a position like closers. There are many ways to draft these teams, which can make dynasty leagues feel more like chess than checkers.

Chapter 3

Starting Pitchers

	SP1	RPV		SP2	RPV		SP3	RPV
1	Tarik Skubal	21%	17	Tanner Bibee	5%	33	Max Fried	8%
2	Zack Wheeler	13%	18	Freddy Peralta	5%	34	Tyler Glasnow	5%
3	Paul Skenes	11%	19	Shota Imanaga	3%	35	Joe Ryan	4%
4	Chris Sale	10%	20	Yoshinobu Yamamoto	3%	36	Sandy Alcantara	4%
5	Logan Gilbert	0%	21	Hunter Brown	3%	37	Shane McClanahan	4%
6	Gerrit Cole	-1%	22	Framber Valdez	3%	38	Justin Steele	1%
7	Dylan Cease	-2%	23	Grayson Rodriguez	1%	39	Jared Jones	0%
8	Blake Snell	-4%	24	Logan Webb	0%	40	Roki Sasaki	0%
9	Michael King	-4%	25	Sonny Gray	0%	41	Kevin Gausman	0%
10	Zac Gallen	-4%	26	Jacob deGrom	-2%	42	Brandon Woodruff	-2%
11	Cole Ragans	-5%	27	Seth Lugo	-2%	43	Luis Gil	-3%
12	Corbin Burnes	-6%	28	Bryce Miller	-3%	44	Christopher Sanchez	-3%
13	George Kirby	-7%	29	Carlos Rodon	-4%	45	Jack Flaherty	-3%
14	Pablo Lopez	-8%	30	Hunter Greene	-4%	46	Bailey Ober	-4%
15	Aaron Nola	-9%	31	Luis Castillo	-4%	47	Bryan Woo	-4%
16	Garrett Crochet	-9%	32	Shohei Ohtani	-6%	48	Tanner Houck	-6%

	SP4	RPV		SP5	RPV
49	Kutter Crawford	6%	65	Shane Bieber	4%
50	Nathan Eovaldi	6%	66	Ranger Suarez	4%
51	Kodai Senga	6%	67	Mitch Keller	4%
52	Sean Manaea	4%	68	Walker Buehler	3%
53	Brandon Pfaadt	3%	69	Luis Severino	3%
54	Reynaldo Lopez	3%	70	Merril Kelly	3%
55	Spencer Schwellenbach	1%	71	MacKenzie Gore	3%
56	Jose Berrios	0%	72	D.J. Herz	3%
57	Nick Pivetta	0%	73	Ryan Weathers	3%
58	Michael Wacha	-2%	74	Bowden Francis	-1%
59	Clarke Schmidt	-2%	75	Jeffrey Springs	-3%
60	Taj Bradley	-2%	76	Cade Povich	-4%
61	Yusei Kikuchi	-3%	77	Ryan Pepiot	-4%
62	Nick Lodolo	-5%	78	Spencer Strider	-4%
63	Robbie Ray	-5%	79	Drew Rasmussen	-6%
64	Shane Baz	-7%	80	Eury Perez	-6%

***Get updated RPV Cheat for one time $5 cost (free updates)
PayPal: FantasyBlackBook@gmail.com or Venmo: @FantasyBlackBook
And include your email address***

Player Profiles and Position Overview

By Joe Pisapia

Once upon a time, pitchers threw 200 innings and were first-round investments. This was especially true in points leagues. The evolution of the fantasy pitcher has gone from that old standard to the great divide between the dominant and the limited to the current state. This new fantasy pitching universe limits even the elite-level arms to a place where the divide is simply not nearly as vast, and the relative position value gaps tighten annually. So, how do we approach this "saved new world" for pitchers? See what I did? That's a literary pun.

Pitchers in 2025 will have higher velocity, equally higher injury risk, and less separation from the herd due to the limitations of younger talent. Only Tarik Skubal ranks as a first-round pick value, in my opinion, and to be fair, he's only had one complete season of dominance. I've been preaching the strategy of buying 1A/#2 arms in bulk for the last few years. This works on two levels. First, you have some cushion for injuries that inevitably strike. Secondly, this allows you to spend early draft capital on offense, which doesn't cycle on the waiver wire as frequently as pitching and is more difficult to keep pace with if you fall behind early. Luckily, plenty of strong values and young pitchers who have been toying with relevance seem poised to take a step forward. Therefore, 2025 could be one of the best value pitching seasons we've seen in drafts in many years.

The Elite

1. **Tarik Skubal, DET:** WOW! Tarik Skubal was a fantasy community darling heading into last year, with the only question being, "Could he be great over a full season?". Well, the answer was a resounding YES! He had 31 starts, 192 IP, 228 K/35 BB, a 2.39 ERA and a 0.92 WHIP. It doesn't get much better than that. Skubal won 18 games for the upstart Tigers. His ERA+ of 170 and 2.50 FIP were the best in the league. No matter how hard you dig, you can't find a blemish on Skubal's 2024 campaign, and for my money, he's clearly the #1 fantasy pitcher heading into 2025.

2. **Zack Wheeler, PHI:** It took him a long time, but Zack Wheeler has become a truly dominant pitcher. He'll be 35 next season and coming off 32 starts, 200 IP, 224 K/52 BB with a 2.56 ERA and a 0.95 WHIP. Wheeler has given fantasy managers back-to-back bangers and he's positioned to be once again one of the top five starters on the board. He led the league in WHIP and H/9 (6.3), and all his deeper stats and splits are sterling. Wheeler is a true ace again heading into 2025.

3. **Paul Skenes, PIT:** We haven't seen this kind of hype around a pitcher since Stephen Strasburg, and Skenes pitched as advertised upon arrival to the show. He made 23 starts, throwing 133 innings with 170 K/32 BB, a 1.96 ERA, and a 0.95 WHIP. Stellar doesn't begin to describe the dominance of Skenes. He threw 160 combined innings between the big leagues and the minors, and he should be good for 175 in theory for 2025. We've seen many pitching phenoms come and go. Many go by the wayside due to injury. Skenes is 6'6" and 235 lbs., so he has the size to handle the workload. His pregame regimen is also intriguing, throwing footballs a la Nolan Ryan. Let's hope the Ryan career path is ahead of him rather than the Strasburg version.

4. **Chris Sale, ATL:** It just feels like the Braves have the Midas Touch when it comes to acquiring starting pitching. Even if you were optimistic about Sale in 2024, I don't think anyone was predicting a Cy Young-worthy campaign. Despite all the injuries in Atlanta affecting the offense and defense, Sale was unbelievably good, winning 18 games with 225 K/39 BB, a 2.38 ERA, and a 1.01 WHIP. By every metric, Sale was dominant—every deep start, peripheral, and split. The only question now is, can he do it again in 2025? At 36, Sale is a harder sell, but I can't justify a reason why he can't other than age, so you must draft him as elite.

5. **Gerrit Cole, NYY:** Gerrit Cole's health was tenuous there for a while, but he managed to hang in there and deliver for the Yankees and fantasy managers alike. His strikeout percentage was still strong but not quite what it was two years ago. Over 95 innings, he has a solid 3.41 ERA, but his xFIP was 3.99, and his walk rate was also the highest since 2018. His home ERA was also high (4.31 vs 2.49 on the road). His first five starts clearly showed Cole getting his footing with a 5.40 ERA. Over his final 12 starts, his 2.76 ERA seemed much more Cole-like. He will be drafted as a fantasy ace somewhere near Round 1 in many drafts. I personally don't like that investment price simply because I want those elite offensive players. However, at 34, Cole still looks a lot like a fantasy ace.

6. **Logan Gilbert: SEA:** I don't care that he had just nine wins in 2024. Gilbert was an absolute stud, and the Mariners' offense was a joke. Gilbert threw 208 innings with a 3.23 ERA, a 0.89 WHIP, and 220 K/37 BB. His BAA was .196. Now, he faded a tad, as his ERA after the break was 4.02 after a dazzling 2.79. However, this was his first time crossing 200 innings so I'm giving him a pass. Do you know why? Almost NO ONE DOES THAT ANYMORE! As Gilbert enters his age 28 season, he's already an elite fantasy rotation option. I feel like his ADP won't be as high as it should be, and that's a mistake in the market you should take advantage of, as all his peripherals were fantastic in 2024.

7. **Dylan Cease, SD:** My biggest regret of the 2024 season is having zero shares of Dylan Cease. The minute he got dealt to the Padres, I kicked myself. Cease had his best all-around season, making 33 starts and winning 14 games with a 3.47 ERA, 1.07 WHIP, and 224 K/65 BB. He did have some months where the ERA shot up above 4, but his deeper metrics by year's end were all under 3.50. Cease will turn 29 this off-season and has had four straight seasons of 32+ starts. There are NOT a lot of pitchers that can claim that sort of durability and are in their prime. As long as that walk rate remains at 3 BB/9, Cease is poised to dominate again and be one of the most dependable rotation investments you can make on draft day.

8. **Michael King, SD:** One of my favorites from last year's Black Book, Michael King gave me everything I hoped for in 2024. That included a 2.95 ERA, 1.19 WHIP, and 201 Ks. He made 30 starts, and his 173 innings should be repeatable in 2025. Fun fact: his FIP (3.08) and xFIP (2.55) mean that last year was no fluke. The Yankees got their Juan Soto and made it to the World Series, but King looks like an ace entering his 30s, and that could be a tough pill to swallow down the road. His 1.57 ERA in September showed 2025 workload should not be an issue. He's an ace in #2 draft stock clothing.

9. **Zac Gallen, ARI:** Gallen missed some time but made 28 starts with a 3.65 ERA, a 1.26 WHIP and a 9.5 K/9. His walk rate did tick up a tad, but Gallen has proven he's one of the better pitchers in baseball over the last few seasons. With Gallen coming off a "down" season by his standards and some others coming off career years, Gallen may actually be more affordable than you think in '25 drafts. He's a great candidate for a 1A pairing at the top of your fantasy rotation if you aren't interested in chasing the very top of the elite tier.

Top Talent

1. **Cole Ragans, KC:** I was high on Cole Ragans last year, with slight concern regarding consistency, and basically, that take ended up being true. Ragans was a strikeout machine, 223 of them in 186 IP. His 3.14 ERA and 1.14 WHIP were terrific, but the 90% LOB rate is unsustainable. Ironically, he was more dominant against RHB than lefties. Ragans did have some rough patches here and there, but we can chalk that up to the growing pains of a full season as a starter. One caveat: his 186 innings were double his previous high, raising his injury risk slightly in 2025, but other than that, it's wheels up for Ragans in '25.

2. **Blake Snell, LAD:** Blake Snell is a box of chocolates; you never know what you're gonna get. After a shaky start to the season, slowed by lingering negotiations, Snell found himself and was lights out down the stretch. His 6.31 ERA over his first eight starts was a distant memory after a 1.45 ERA over his final 12. Snell is still in his prime and carries elite-level strikeout potential. It seems he will always have stretches where you question why you drafted him, but he inevitably reminds you and rewards you. You just have to stay the course. The dude can be simply unhittable at times. However, the annual hiccup stretch keeps him from being "elite." Although, pitching for the juggernaut Dodgers could push him to that territory despite any inconsistencies.

3. **Corbin Burnes, ARI:** The Orioles went all in with Corbin Burnes, and he looked like the Cy Young favorite in the first half, posting a 2.43 ERA and 1.04 WHIP. But in the second half, Burnes had a more pedestrian 3.69 ERA. His strikeout rate continued to decline for the fourth straight season, and he was not the same dominant force he was in '21-'22. Still, he remains a front-line fantasy starter and in his prime. There are no glaring indicators of rapid decline, and his FIP and xFIP are in line with his ERA. Perhaps the K rate decline is part of his evolution as a pitcher, but as a fantasy manager, you long for those days. He is a strong value pay ace who should see plenty of run support in Arizona.

4. **George Kirby, SEA:** Kirby won 14 games for the Mariners with a 3.53 ERA, 1.07 WHIP, and 179 K/ 23 BB. Kirby's absurdly low walk rate makes him so appealing. His numbers were slightly less dominant on the road (3.91 ERA), but that's really the only blemish on a sterling season. Turning 27 in 2025, Kirby will look to copy and paste his '24 stats, which are worth bidding aggressively on for the sake of your fantasy team. There's a chance he has an even higher level of performance in him, but the benchmark is already brilliant. He's a prime long-term asset.

5. **Pablo Lopez, MIN:** All last season, I kept screaming BUY Pablo Lopez because his ERA was far higher than the deeper numbers suggested it should be. Well, it eventually landed at 4.08 after 32 starts, with a 1.19 WHIP and 198 K/41 BB. His xERA last year was 3.70, the FIP was 3.65, and the xFIP was just 3.36. Lopez had a lot of bad luck, resulting in a first-half ERA above 5, but clearly, he was not the issue, and once again, I'm buying aggressively in 2025. As long as that wicked 5:1 strikeout to walk rate holds, Lopez is going to be a tremendous investment.

6. **Aaron Nola, PHI:** Four straight seasons of 32 or more starts with 180+ innings makes Nola one of the great workhorses of fantasy baseball. His K/9 declined over that time, but it remained at around 9 K/9, and his BB/9 was still around 2. The xERA and FIP were a bit higher than his actual 3.57 mark, but all his home/road and pre/post splits were solid. Nola is one of the better pitching investments you can make. In a sea of guys who can't stay healthy, Nola delivers the rare combination of quality and quantity.

7. **Tanner Bibee, CLE:** I was cautiously optimistic Tanner Bibee could become an ace when Shane Bieber went down, and he stepped into that void and flourished. He made 31 starts, compiling a 3.47 ERA and a 1.12 WHIP with 187 K/44 BB. The extra playoff innings on top of the career high of innings could rear their ugly head in 2025, but most pitchers are risky anyway, so you might as well go after him. All his underlying peripherals were sound. The one knock was the home 4.115 ERA compared to his 2.76 road mark. Bibee looks like a strong option in 2025.

8. **Freddy Peralta, MIL:** Peralta delivered his best season in 2024, crossing 170 IP for the first time, delivering his second consecutive 200-strikeout season. There were questions about whether Peralta could be "the man" for the Brewers with Corbin Burnes gone and Brandon Woodruff hurt. Well, he answered those questions and should be considered a strong front of the rotation fantasy arm in all formats in 2025. A few notes: his 3.68 ERA did come with a 3.88 xERA, 4.16 FIP, and 39.3 xFIP. That means his ERA could be higher in '25. Also, his .167 BABIP was incredibly low. Still, Peralta remains a strong investment.

9. **Shota Imanaga, CHC:** Last season, I made the declarative statement that Shota Imanaga would be the better draft investment than his fellow import Yoshinobu Yamamoto, which turned out to be true. Imanaga was older but seemed like the more durable sure thing with the better risk/reward ratio. He made 29 starts with a 2.91 ERA, 1.02 WHIP, and 174 K/28 BB while winning 15 games. His home/road and pre/post break splits were all strong. The only knock on Imanaga is that his FIP and xFIP suggest that 2.91 ERA will likely shoot up to the 3.75 range in 2025. Still, Imanaga is a "pitcher," which has become a lost art form in this era. He finds the outs in lineups and knows how to mix his pitchers to keep hitters off balance. The league never really adjusted to him, and I'm bullish about him in 2025.

10. **Yoshinobu Yamamoto, LAD:** The Dodgers broke the bank for Yamamoto, but he only made 18 starts due to injury. The good news is that he was 7-2 with a 3.00 ERA, a 1.11 WHIP, and 105 K/22 BB over those games. The quality was on full display, but if he's going to be drafted as aggressively as last season, he needs to deliver quantity as well. All the numbers check out, and the 28-year-old Yamamoto could have a very bright future. His smaller frame was the biggest concern coming over from Japan, and so far, that concern remains. Still, he has huge upside pitching for the Dodgers.

11. **Hunter Brown, HOU:** After a disastrous start (11.84 ERA in April), Hunter Brown had a course correction and turned in a strong 2024 campaign and a 3.49 ERA. Brown was dazzling down the stretch with a 2.28 ERA and a 1.14 WHIP over his final 12 starts. It's exciting to think of what his line may look like with six consistent months instead of five. We'll have to wait and see. His splits were strong, and his 10 ERA with RISP was the only other blemish. That's got to get cleaned up if he's going to jump another tier.

12. **Framber Valdez, HOU:** Valdez remains one of the more underrated pitchers in fantasy. Extremely consistent and reliable, Valdez is a guy you can draft, set, and forget. Those kinds of assets are few and far between in the pitching department nowadays. Valdez did have an injury hiccup early in the year, but he finished with a flourish, posting a 1.96 ERA, 0.88 WHIP, and 87 K over his final 78 IP. He's the rock of the Astros rotation and the ideal #2 fantasy starter.

13. **Garrett Crochet, BOS:** The lone bright spot in a cave of darkness for the White Sox was Garrett Crochet, who realized his full potential in 2024. His 12.9 K/9 was incredible, as was his 2.0 BB/9. Over 32 starts, he posted a 3.58 ERA and a 1.06 WHIP. He was absolutely filthy. His innings were limited down the stretch, and he totaled 146, so hopefully, there will be no issues in 2025 going for 175+. The White Sox are awful, though (he won just six games in '24). Crochet on the Red Sox certainly boosts his win potential and he has front line ace potential written all over him. It's now about health and building innings.

14. **Grayson Rodriguez, BAL:** Before a lat injury ended Grayson Rodriguez's 2024 campaign, he showed the baseball world why the hype was legit. Over 20 starts, he was 13-4 over 116 IP, with 130 K/36 BB and a 1.24 WHIP. Normally, lat issues are tricky, but with the whole off-season, he should be ready to rock. He'll turn 25 this year and remain a high-level long and short-term asset. The injury may even hurt his redraft stock a bit, making him a very desirable investment. The true "breakout" season is coming, and it could be as soon as 2025.

15. **Logan Webb, SF:** Webb has been a fantasy workhorse these last few years, but something seemed a little off this spring and never quite got back to the 2023 levels we were hoping for last season. Webb threw 200 innings again for the second straight year and posted a 3.47 ERA (2.95 FIP) and a 1.23 WHIP. However, his K/9 dropped from 8.1 to 7.6, and the BB/9 jumped from 1.3 to 2.2, as did the H/9 from 8.4 to 8.9. All of these are acceptable, but his margin for error became thinner for a guy without true power stuff. Webb remains a safe investment for now, taking the ball every fifth day, which is extremely valuable in our current pitching climate.

16. **Sonny Gray, STL:** The Cardinals rotation was a hot mess, save Sonny Gray who was a strikeout machine in 2024. His 11 K/9 was his highest since 2019, and he walked just 39 over 166 innings. Gray had a 3.84 ERA, but his 3.12 FIP and 2.82 xFIP mean that number could drop in '25. Gray's career has had some highs and lows, but he seems to have settled into a nice run these last few seasons and is one of the more cost-effective front-of-the-rotation fantasy pitchers you'll find. One note: Gray did have right forearm flexor tendinitis at the season's end, but reports have been positive on that front for him this off-season.

17. **Seth Lugo, KC:** If there was one true breakout from last year's Black Book pitching section, it was Seth Lugo. However, I must admit he surpassed my lofty expectations. Lugo threw 206 IP over 33 starts, with a 3.00 ERA, 1.08 WHIP, and a terrific 181 K/ 48 BB ratio. He faced a league-high 836 batters and was a rock for the Royals and a league winner for fantasy managers. I expect his ERA to regress to around the mid-3 range based on his 3.72 xERA and 3.83 xFIP. That should keep him close to the front of most fantasy rotations. Can he repeat? I think he can. And that question looming for most fantasy players should keep his cost relatively reasonable.

18. **Bryce Miller, SEA:** Man, Seattle's rotation is good! Miller threw 180 innings over 31 starts with a 2.94 ERA, 0.98 WHIP, and 171 K/45 BB. Batters hit just .200 against him, but the deeper stats suggest a slight jump in ERA year over year to the mid-3 range. That still puts Miller in a great spot to be a #3 fantasy starter. Now, if his K/9 rates climb to his lofty minor league range (well over 10 K/9), then Miller could launch into the stratosphere. Miller is a substantial value with upside for more, making him a great buy in 2025.

The Wild Cards

1. **Roki Sasaki, LAD:** The rich got richer! The most coveted Japanese pitcher became a Dodger this off-season which assuredly will inflate his stock to nearly untenable standards. Sasaki is a flamethrowing 23-year-old who has dominated the Japanese league for the last two seasons. Sasaki struck out 129 hitters and walked just 32 in 111 innings. His 2.35 ERA and 1.04 WHIP indicate there's nothing left for him to prove overseas. At 6'2", he has good size, but he's still very slender, and we all know the rigors of the major league schedule can be an adjustment. The redraft ADP vs. ROI will be fascinating. In dynasty leagues, the aggressive investment will be more appropriate.

2. **Tomoyuki Sugano, BAL:** Sugano is 35 years old, coming off another solid year in Japan. His career K/9 of 7.7 is underwhelming and although you could look for him to perhaps be an asset over the first few months of 2025, but the second time around the league without "punch out" caliber stuff could be more challenging.

Solid Options

1. **Carlos Rodon, NYY:** Rodon nearly matched his career high in innings last year with 175. He won 16 games with a 3.96 ERA, 1.22 WHIP, and 195 K/57 BB. His 4.39 FIP was a tad scary, but considering he turned in a career-high 32 starts, managers will take it. So why is he not "Top Talent"? For starters, his injury history is far too long and storied. Secondly, his 4.68 road ERA (3.11 at home) made him a tricky weekly start. Rodon will always be a dangerous investment, and the adage "don't draft a team for last year" rings true here. Still, I can't ignore his strong 2024 altogether. Rodon, as a #1, is not ideal. As a #2 starter, I'm less scared. As a #3, I'm excited.

2. **Hunter Greene, CIN:** Big strides last year for Hunter Greene! He's primed to ascend the ranks in 2025 after a 2.75 ERA, a 1.02 WHIP, and a 3:1 K/BB ratio. His 10 K/9 rate is elite, and his walk rate has lowered a tad year over year to a more manageable pace. His 5.7 H/9 showed he's one of the toughest pitchers to square up in the game today, and his HR rate was cut in half! Elbow inflammation robbed us of a full Greene year, but he did return at season's end to prove he was

healthy. Now, all he has to do is stay healthy, and Greene could very well become a fantasy ace in 2025. At 26, he's one of the most promising young pitchers in the game.

3. **Luis Castillo, SEA:** Some of my concerns from last year's FIP data came home to roost in 2024 for Castillo. His ERA jumped from 3.34 to 3.64, and yet again, his peripherals are slightly troubling. The xERA (3.94), FIP (3.91), and xFIP (3.82) could mean that ERA will climb another tick in 2025. However, Castillo remains a pitcher who strikes out a batter per inning. He has to improve versus LHB, who held him to a 4.90 ERA, if he's going to reclaim his highest value. I'm not ready to "red flag" Castillo yet, but he's a riskier investment heading into this season than last.

4. **Max Fried, NYY:** I had health concerns about Fried coming into 2024, but he made 29 starts and threw 174 innings with 166 K/57 BB, a 3.25 ERA, and a 1.16 WHIP. He struggled in the summer (4.50 ERA in July, 5.03 in August) but rebounded in September (2.17). His home/road and per/post break splits were all sound, and his deeper numbers aligned with his ERA. Fried remains a solid front-of-the-rotation fantasy starter in his prime, but he's not a fantasy ace, no matter how much he got paid this off-season by the Yankees. We'll see how he adjusts to New York. The forearm issues are still floating in my mind.

5. **Joe Ryan, MIN:** I had high hopes for Joe Ryan in 2024, but he didn't quite reach expectations. He made just 23 starts due to a Grade 2 teres major strain. He was 7-7 over 135 IP with a 3.60 ERA and 0.99 WHIP. The hope is that he has the entire off-season now to recover, and in 2025, he can make a run at 30 starts for the first time in his career as he heads into his age-29 season. His secondary numbers all align with his strong ERA, and it's just a matter of health for him to have a true breakout season. Perhaps we were only a year delayed from that reality, or Ryan is a guy who will tease on that promise and never quite deliver. I would still be bidding on the promise and be optimistic when it comes to Ryan in 2025.

6. **Justin Steele, CHC:** After starting the season late, Steele ended up making 24 starts over 134 innings with a 3.07 ERA, a 1.10 WHIP, and 135 K/37 BB. All his deeper stats are very strong, and Steele has been one of my favorite values for the last two seasons. He'll likely remain a value this season, too, based upon his teammate Shota Imanaga getting all the press and the injury bug once again biting him. If Steele can put elbow tendinitis behind him and make 32 starts, he'll be a fantastic fantasy investment this season. He's not without risk, but the ADP should be friendly enough to invest.

7. **Jared Jones, PIT:** The 23-year-old Jones started the season on fire with an ERA of 2.88 in April and a WHIP of 0.96. He had 98 strikeouts and 27 walks over his first 91 innings. Unfortunately, a lat issue put him on the shelf, and he struggled to regain his elite pre-break form. The 5.96 ERA over his last six starts says it all. His 5.86 ERA on the road was also problematic. Jones' previous high of 122 innings in 2022 was only slightly surpassed with 131 combined in '24. So, if there is a silver lining, he was probably going to be limited in innings anyway last season, as the Pirates really limited him down the stretch. He should be looking at 150 innings for 2025, and Jones is a worthwhile gamble this season based on how strong he started. Now, we just need a complete, healthy season.

8. **Christopher Sanchez, PHI:** Last season, Sanchez blossomed into a terrific starting pitcher. He made 31 starts over 181 innings and had 153 K/44 BB with a 3.32 ERA and a 1.24 WHIP. In roto leagues, his deeper stats suggest his ERA could have been closer to 3. Despite the fact his K rate is slightly less than top-notch, he won 11 games and was a great value. His ADP will be significantly higher this year as he enters his prime at age 28. The one concern is the massive home (2.21 ERA)/road splits (5.02 ERA). That makes him a much better season-long roto investment than a weekly head-to-head option. He struggled in July and August but finished with a flourish in September with a 2.47 ERA over five starts. Sanchez now has to prove that his 2024 wasn't a fluke, and I don't think it was.

9. **Bailey Ober, MIN:** Ober made some big strides forward in 2024, so I can forgive the fatigue of a 5.32 ERA over his last 23.2 innings. The FIP numbers suggest his 3.76 ERA could be more like 4.00 in 2025, but his 9 K.9 and 2.2 BB/9 are an asset in any fantasy league, as was his 1.00 WHIP. Ober is entering his prime, and although we've been waiting a while for him to reach his potential, it feels like patience is finally being rewarded.

10. **Bryan Woo, SEA:** 2024 was a season of ups and downs and injuries for Bryan Woo. However, when the dust settled, you could see a guy on the rise. Woo threw 121 innings over 22 starts with a 2.89 ERA, 0.90 WHIP, and 101 K/13 BB. If his strikeout rate ticks up a bit, which could happen based on his minor league track record, and that walk rate stays the same, Woo could be a cheaper version of his rotation mate Bryce Miller. Woo carries more risk but at a lower cost. That makes him a fun investment in 2025. Let's see if he's ready to jump over 150 innings this season.

11. **Tanner Houck, BOS:** Tanner Houck delivered on his sleeper promise in 2024, delivering a 3:1 K/BB rate and a 3.12 ERA. His 178 IP was a jump from the previous season's 106 IP. That can be a cause for concern. Case in point, his second-half ERA jumped to 4.23 after a 2.54 first half. Still, Houck did enough for me to be a draft day target as a solid middle-rotation starter. Perhaps most encouraging is Houck's xERA, xFIP, and FIP, which aligned with his low 3 ERA, and his home/road splits were equal. That all bodes well for a repeat of his solid '24 campaign in 2025. A great value play!

12. **Kutter Crawford, BOS:** Crawford had a lot of buzz last off-season and delivered on some of the hype. Over 183 IP, he had 175K/51 BB and a 1.12 WHIP. His 4.36 ERA was a tad disappointing but not far off from his xERA, FIP, and xFIP. It was really a tale of two halves, though, for Crawford, who entered the break with a 3.00 ERA over 114 innings but had a 6.59 ERA over his final 69.2 innings. Could it be the jump from 129 to 180 innings? Sure. Could the league have figured him out, and does he need to adjust in response? Absolutely. Crawford was borderline "red flag" material, but he was so good in the first half that I'm going to have faith he can pace himself better in 2025.

13. **Nathan Eovaldi, TEX:** Eovaldi's 170 innings were his highest mark since 2021. Over those 29 starts, he had a 3.80 ERA, 1.11 WHIP, and 166 K/44 BB. He'll be entering his age-35 season, so there's reason to pause despite his being consistent over the last five years. Also, his ERA in the second half was 4.88 compared to 2.97 before the All-Star Game, and LHB gave him trouble. Eovaldi is better suited to season-long roto formats where his missed starts and career stage are easier to bear than in a weekly head-to-head format. I'd rather be drafting younger pitchers in this same range with more upside, but if you get stuck with ole Nate, he's decent enough in 2025 redraft scenarios.

14. **Kodai Senga, NYM:** Senga's 2024 season never got off the ground. First, a shoulder injury cost him three months, and then he returned only to suffer a calf injury, which cost him the rest of the season. He came back for the playoff run with some mixed results, but the velocity was good, so clearly more rust than anything. Senga is pitching for a good team and has elite-level strikeout potential. If he checks out in spring training, you should buy in 2025.

15. **Brandon Pfaadt, ARI:** On the surface, that 4.71 ERA looks terrifying, but his 3.75 xERA, 3.61 FIP, and 3.58 xFIP make him one of the more attractive sleepers in 2025. Pfaadt has a topflight strikeout rate of 9 K/9 and a BB/9 around 2. At 26, he has all the earmarks of a great buy low in 2025 across all formats. He even sliced his HR rate in half! The 181 innings were a leap, but considering he's turning 26, Pfaadt is a worthwhile gamble who could easily jump a tier this season.

16. **Reynaldo Lopez, ATL:** Lopez came out of nowhere and saved a lot of fantasy rotations from the waiver wire. When you dig deeper into his FIP and xERA, they suggest he should have had a mid-3 ERA, not the 1.99 ERA he delivered. However, that doesn't make him a complete red flag because his walk rate dropped, and his strikeout rate was above average. Lopez seems to have found himself in Atlanta, and it would be tough not to envision him in the rotation. The wheels never fell off, and he had a sub-2 ERA over the final two months of the season. One would expect some regression in '25, but not enough to steer away him in drafts.

17. **Spencer Schwellenbach, ATL:** The 24-year-old gave the Braves a much-needed jolt in the back of their rotation in 2024. After posting an ERA in the high-5 range over his first 30 innings, Schwellenbach settled down and had a 2.73 ERA over his final 79 innings. His 3.35 ERA was not a mirage when you see the FIP stats, and his 9.2 K/9 and 1.6 BB/9 mean he could become a very strong investment in 2025. The league will probably adjust to him, so the challenge will be adjusting back. However, if the finish is an indicator of things to come, Schwellenbach could be a breakout star in 2025.

18. **Jose Berrios, TOR:** It was a copy and paste for Jose Berrios year over year. Another 3.60 ERA, a third straight 32-start season, and a second straight year of a sub 1.20 WHIP. The strikeout rate dropped from 8 to 7 K/9, which isn't great. His 4.72 FIP is also troubling. However, in season-long fantasy, the 31-year-old Berrios is probably a set-and-forget starter. In head-to-head formats, just play his matchups carefully. He's not a "dominant" pitcher, and his ERA was 4.00 in road starts. Your prototypical #3 starter who will give you the occasional #1 performance, the occasional bomb, but mostly just average more often than not. His durability is probably his best ability.

19. **Nick Pivetta, FA:** Pivetta has evolved into a league-average starter with a nice 10 K/9. His ERA is always doomed to be around 4, as he still gives up too many longballs. He did make progress on that walk rate, lowering it year over year from 3.2 to 2.2. If that holds, Pivetta will be a very strong 2025 fantasy arm. Pivetta is in his prime, and the Red Sox look to be competitive, so bank on 170 Ks, double-digit wins, and a 4 ERA. Just beware of strong right-handed hitting lineups against him (.304 BA/.814 OPS v RHB) and on the road (4.42 road ERA).

20. **Michael Wacha, KC:** Wacha has never been an elite strikeout guy, but he put together his best season in years with the Royals in 2024. He made 29 starts (if you can believe it) with a 3.35 ERA and 1.19 WHIP, and he won 13 games. His 3:1 K/BB rate is the secret sauce. His xERA and xFIP were around 4, so ERA regression is likely coming. Still, his 2.79 second-half ERA is very encouraging, and maybe Wacha has finally landed in a good place, considering that once upon a time, we expected this type of season to be the standard, not the outlier. Wacha is a nice value in '25.

21. **Taj Bradley, TB:** Taj Bradley was lights out to start the year with a 2.90 ERA before the AS break. But his final 13 starts gave way to a 5.30 mark. You can argue the fatigue factor of his first full big-league season or the league caught up with him. Regardless, Bradley is now at a fork in the road. Is he the dominant strikeout artist or the inefficient guy who will kill your peripherals? Approaching 2025, I would like to give him the benefit of the doubt that he can settle into more consistency. It could also help to have some healthy big names around him for a change to ease the burden of carrying the rotation as he did for most of the year. He's not a finished product, but certainly an intriguing one.

22. **Clarke Schmidt, NYY:** Clarke Schmidt turned a quietly strong 2024. He made 16 starts and had a 2.85 ERA, 1.18 WHIP, and a 9.8 K/9. The FIP was 3.58, but we'll gladly take that over a full season. At 28, Schmidt made great progress year over year despite the walk rate ticking up a tad. Fun fact: he allowed three or fewer runs in every start except his final one. The Yankees will again be a strong team, so Schmidt should rack up wins and hopefully settle into a mid-3 ERA over 30 starts in 2025. Hot take: I could see Schmidt being a better investment at ADP than his rotation mate, Luis Gil.

23. **Yusei Kikuchi, LAA:** At 33, Kikuchi had a dazzling contract year. His 206 strikeouts and 1.20 WHIP were career-bests. Weird fact: he had a 5.36 ERA in day games, so keep this night owl out of your lineups in daylight hours. He got stronger as the year went on, with a 3.51 ERA and 1.05 WHIP over his final 12 starts. Lefties have a way of being late bloomers, and that may very well be the case for Kikuchi, who's been around for a while and is just now starting to realize his potential. Unfortunately, the Angels will hold back any win potential.

24. **Sean Manaea, NYM:** A change in arm angle turned journeyman Sean Manaea into one of the best pitchers in the National League after the all-star break. Over his 32 starts, he posted 184 K/63 BB, a 3.47 ERA, and a 1.08 WHIP. The xERA and FIP numbers suggest some slight ERA regression is coming, but if he makes 30 starts with a 3.75 ERA and maintains the K/BB ratio, he will be a good draft pick in '25. Manaea resigning with the Mets gave him the best chance to repeat his success.

25. **Nick Lodolo, CIN:** Injury after injury kept Lodolo from breaking out in 2024. His season ended due to a finger injury, but he should have a normal off-season. Lodolo offered a 9.5 K/9 and a 1.20 WHIP when he was on the hill. Sure, the 4.79 ERA was high, but his FIP stats suggest that number should have been more like 4 flat. He'll be 27 this year, and lefties typically take a bit longer to develop consistency. Lodolo is one of the more intriguing later draft picks at starting pitcher because he had the pedigree and strikeout potential to make a giant leap forward sooner than later. I'm investing at the current ADP, and you should, too.

26. **Robbie Ray. SF:** Ray returned from TJ late in the season and continued to be a strikeout beast with 43 in his 30 innings. At times, he will struggle with control, but one thing is certain, he will get you Ks, and now he has a new elbow! In formats where strikeouts matter more, make him a target. At 33, he's got a few good years left in the tank.

Returning From TJ

1. **Shohei Ohtani, LAD:** The greatest baseball player we've ever seen will return to the mound in 2025. In leagues where he's one player, and you get both his bat and arm, he's far and away the most valuable asset in all of fantasy baseball. In leagues where he's a stand-alone pitcher or hitter (dumb for the record), he's an elite-level strikeout artist (11.4 K/9 in '23) who, at times, can be a tad wild (3.8 BB/9 in '23). Luckily, he makes up for that walk rate with a career .200 BAA and a 0.98 WHIP. His 166 innings in 2022 were his career-high mark, and one would imagine he would be earmarked for something close or below that in 2025, returning from surgery. Although he is superhuman, so going over that total can't be ruled out. Because he plays every day and pitches, his injury risk is, of course, higher than any other player based on exposure alone. However, Ohtani is so dominant at everything that he's worth the risk.

2. **Shane McClanahan, TB:** When we last saw McClanahan, he looked like a Cy Young candidate. Unfortunately, that was 2023. In 2025, McClanahan should have a clear path ahead as he looks to regain his dominant form. His 3.02 career ERA and 1.10 WHIP bode well for the 28-year-old being a fantasy ace yet again. At times, some pitchers struggle early to get a feel for pitching in games again after such a long layoff, but his elite-level upside remains. His career high in innings was 166, so I would expect a cap of 175 in the regular season as the Rays look to get back to being a perennial playoff team once again. One small note, prior to injury, his 3.90 FIP was a gap between his 3.29 ERA in 2023. This may be indicative of his health, but he should be drafted at a fair enough discount not to let that number hamper your interest in him. More good news: he was working off the mound already in August. Patience will be rewarded.

3. **Sandy Alcantara, MIA:** One of the most consistent pitchers in fantasy, Sandy Alcantara clearly was not right in 2023. He soldiered through 184 innings after delivering 200+ in back-to-back prior seasons. Now, Alcantara has a new elbow, and hopefully, the now 20-year-old workhorse can get back to those 30-start/200-inning seasons. Alcantara has never been a "dominant" strikeout guy but instead a throwback pitcher who knows how to get outs in lineups and work deep into games. The Marlins will be terrible again, but there's a good chance he will be shipped to a contender if he has no setbacks. I know this because the Marlins have said they won't be dealing him. See what I did there? He was already throwing bullpens and live BP in September, so he's not quite as far along as Shane McClanahan, but he should be ready to open '25 on time.

4. **Brandon Woodruff, MIL:** Shoulder capsule surgery is tricky, especially for a power pitcher like Brandon Woodruff. His career ERA (3.10) among qualified starting pitchers in franchise history and seventh in strikeouts (788) means the rotation spot will be there if Woodruff is healthy enough to fill it. I feel far less confident in Woodruff than I do in McClanahan or Alcantara. The good news is that his ADP will be cheaper, and the team he's returning to is a good one that won their division. At his best, he's a 10 K/9 guy who will flirt with an ERA around 3 and a WHIP around 1.00. That's elite-level stuff. My instincts are he will be a fun early best ball asset, and as draft season rolls on and he looks better in the Spring, his ADP will rise significantly. As long as the price doesn't become untenable, Woodruff is a league-winning type of investment. Just make sure you have the depth to back him up.

5. **Eury Perez, MIA:** Eury Perez was simply dazzling upon his MLB debut. At just 21, he made 19 starts in 2023 with a 3.15 ERA, a 1.12 WHIP, and 108 K/31 BB. But then came Tommy John, sigh. The bright side is that he had his surgery last April and would likely be on an innings cap anyway at his age. My estimation is somewhere around June 1, we see Perez, giving you four months of 5-inning starts with strikeout upside. Perez is more valuable in keeper/dynasty scenarios than redraft leagues, but he also carries some redraft weight. You just have to manage expectations as the Marlins manage his workload.

6. **Spencer Strider, ATL:** When healthy, Strider is one of the elite strikeout artists in baseball. There's a chance that things will go well during his recovery, and he will show up late in 2025, but setbacks often occur, and Strider's 2025 value is completely unknown at this point.

7. **Shane Bieber, CLE:** What a shame. Bieber was dominant in the early going and looked like his old self. I'd be buying cheap in keeper/dynasty. It would be realistic for him to return in late June, but that's without any setbacks. If you can stash him in a league with deep IL spots, you could.

8. **Johan Oviedo, PIT:** Johan Oviedo showed some glimpses in 2023 of being a decent starter for the Pirates. He pitched 177.2 innings, the eighth-most in a single season from any Pirates starter over the last decade. Unfortunately, he missed all of 2024 with Tommy John. That rotation changed quite a bit over that period with some bright young stars, so a starting role may have to be earned. Oviedo seems more like a second-half contributor or waiver wire add.

9. **Lucas Giolito, BOS:** Giolito underwent an internal brace procedure to repair the UCL in his right elbow, and this was not his first elbow injury. His return to form is tenuous at best. When he's right, Giolito is a guy that can rack up strikeouts. Considering his history, he's a flier right now, but he is just 30.

Red Flags

1. **Jacob deGrom, TEX:** The last time Jacob deGrom threw more than 90 innings was pre-pandemic in 2019. Recovered from TJ surgery, deGrom made three appearances late in 2024 and looked pretty good (10.2 IP, 14 K, 1 BB, 1.69 ERA, 1.12 WHIP). We all know the upside of deGrom is the best pitcher in baseball. The downside is he gives you nothing on the IL. Chris Sale's journey back to prominence is an interesting comparison; however, his injuries were more varied. deGrom stock is all about cost. As a fantasy ace, I can't get there at 37 years old. As a #2 in a shallow league, I'm curious. As a #3 starter, I'm buying. My concern is that the hype gets out of control in March, and the cost becomes difficult to bear. Best ball, go for broke!

2. **Tyler Glasnow, LAD:** Glasnow was a strikeout machine, but then injury struck again. Elbow inflammation cost him the last third of the season, and as of October, he had yet to resume any throwing program. Glasnow remains an annual risk/reward guy, but at 31, he's never thrown more than 130 big league innings in a season. If he ever threw 175 innings, he'd easily strike out 200+ and win 15+ games. No matter how good the off-season goes, or spring goes, or the first half goes, he'll always be a high-injury risk arm.

3. **Luis Gil, NYY:** Before you get mad at me, let me say Luis Gil was a league winner in 2024 that exceeded all lofty expectations. He won 15 games over 29 starts and struck out 177 in 151 IP with a 1.19 WHIP. Now, as we look closer, his 77 walks led the league. His xERA was 3.83, FIP was 4.14, and xFIP was 4.36. Not to mention, his LOB% was a tad high and BABIP a tad low. I'm not saying Gil is a pass, but I am saying this was a HUGE jump in innings for him in one season, which typically leads to problems in the following season. That ERA jumped from 3.17 before the break to 4.20 afterward. It was a magical '24 season. If you draft Gil, you had better back yourself up because some glaring red flags could bode poorly for him in 2025. Don't hate me; I have your best interests at heart.

4. **Kevin Gausman, TOR:** I give you the monthly ERAs of Kevin Gausman in 2024: April 4.50, May 3.76, June 5.65, July 3.45, Aug 2.89, Sept 2.25. Exhausted yet? His elite-level double-digit K/9 rate fell all the way to 8 K/9 while his walk rate increased for a second straight year. The 3.83 ERA hides a 4.77 xERA and a 4.22 xFIP. Basically, he's putting more guys on, becoming more hittable, and striking out fewer batters. Either there was an injury he hid all year, or he's in decline. Either way, Gausman is a major red flag for 2025.

5. **Walker Buehler, BOS:** What seemed like a can't-miss guy can't seem to find the plate. Buehler's injuries have been his undoing, and although he's only 30, his 5.38 ERA over 16 starts leaves far too many questions and not enough answers. You can pretend he was "better in September," but it still wasn't good. Velocity may have returned, but the results have not. Although, he did have some nice post-season outings. His pitches still have some movement, but he must look really sharp this spring to get me excited enough to take a flier on him in 2025. Boston gives him a chance to find his old form with a competitive roster.

6. **Jack Flaherty, FA:** Flaherty has been awful since 2021. Then suddenly, 2024 hits, and he threw up a 2.98 ERA over 18 starts with the Tigers. Sure, health was not an issue, and maybe the Tigers got him to make some much-needed tweaks to his approach. He then gets dealt to LA, where the ERA rises to the FIP of 3.50, but the walk rate starts to rise. He had some good moments in the postseason (and some dicey ones). The 29-year-old Flaherty did all of this in a contract year. Crazy right? Maybe Flaherty is a guy who has truly turned a corner and regained the form that made him a bright young star once upon a time in St. Louis. Then again, he could be a guy who crushed your hopes and dreams the two years prior. If he comes at a modest SP3 price tag on draft day, I'm open to finding out which one shows up in 2025.

7. **Ranger Suarez, PHI:** Another Philly pitcher who emerged as a strong starter in 2024 was Ranger Suarez. But as good as he was in the first half (2.76 ERA/1.04 WHIP), he was as bad after the break (5.72 ERA/1.71 WHIP). This leaves Suarez's 2025 prospects in limbo. It wasn't a jump and innings to blame because he had crossed 150 previously, but he did miss some time with a back issue. However, his troubles began before that. Suarez is a gamble in 2025, and as a back-end starter, you could do worse. You could also do better.

8. **Mitch Keller, PIT:** Keller is usually good for a few months, but then the wheels come off, and he crashes and burns. His career 5.03 ERA after the All-Star Break makes him the ultimate sell-off come July. Even last year, Keller was cruising with a 3.47 ERA and a 1.25 over his first 19 starts. Then, kaboom! Over his final 12 starts, Keller had a droppable 5.70 ERA and 1.41 WHIP. He has decent enough swing-and-miss stuff and doesn't walk too many, but he's far too hittable and fails to work out of jams. Keller is a back-end starter, and if you do draft, you need to become independent of him before Independence Day.

9. **Drew Rasmussen, TB**: Rasmussen made his return from TJ late in 2024, throwing 28 innings with 35 K/6 BB and a 2.83 ERA. The Rays rotation would be incredible in 2025, and Rasmussen may be one of the more cost-effective ways to get a part of it. However, this was his third major UCL repair surgery. He's not guaranteed a rotation spot, and his history could ticket him to the bullpen to limit his exposure. He's an asset I would want on my roster regardless, as I think he could make starts in '25, but you have to be realistic and realize he could have limitations.

10. **Jeffrey Springs, ATH:** Springs did return in 2024 from his TJ, but only to have his season shut down in September with elbow fatigue. That leaves his 2025 status in limbo. The 31-year-old had a 3.27 ERA, 1.36 WHIP, and 37K/11 BB over just 33 innings in 2024. Springs looked incredible before his TJ surgery, but now, heading into 2025, doubt will linger if he can regain that kind of form. As a cheap investment, he's worth it. The trouble is, I fear some will be more aggressive than they should, and that could make the price tag less appealing. The fact Tampa dealt him is also troublesome.

11. **Merril Kelly, ARI:** Kelly missed most of 2024 with a shoulder issue. The 70 innings he contributed were decent, with a 4 ERA and a 1.17 WHIP, but he's never been a strikeout artist, and he's turning 37 next year. He's not a complete "stay away" but more of a "proceed with caution."

12. **Yu Darvish, SD:** When we saw Yu Darvish in 2024, he was decent. He had 16 starts, a 3.31 ERA, and a 1.07 WHIP with respectable K/BB rates. The trouble is, he's pushing 40, and the reason for his absence was elbow inflammation. Not the best combination.

13. **Nestor Cortes MIL:** Cortes was diagnosed with a left elbow flexor strain in late September. His 174 IP and 3.77 ERA seem like a nice investment, but I can't get past that elbow issue looming. I'm fading Cortes. The off-season deal was a downgrade for him.

14. **Charlie Morton, BAL:** He'll be 41 next season, and despite the fact that he had a decent 2024 season, I'm not in the business of drafting pitchers of a certain age. His strikeout rate is in decline, and his mid-4 xERA and FIP are warning signs. I respect the veteran a great deal, but I would rather be taking shots late on upside guys than Morton, who had a 1.47 WHIP after the break.

15. **Brady Singer, KC:** I didn't care for the year's finish. A 5.53 ERA in August and a 5.67 in September don't make me feel warm and fuzzy about 2025. It wasn't like he hadn't thrown back-to-back 150-inning seasons before jumping to 179 in 2024. His 3.94 FIP and brutal finish make him a suspect asset in 2025.

16. **Justin Verlander, SF:** This is what happens when you stay at the dance too long. A "red flag" guy last year in the Black Book, Verlander was, as feared, bad. His 5.48 ERA and 1.38 WHIP were dark chapters in the story of a brilliant career. He was even left off the playoff roster, YIKES! At 42 years old with neck issues, h's now with the Giants, but I would steer clear outside of a extremely late dart throw.

17. **Max Scherzer, TOR:** Another 40-year-old free agent, Scherzer, continues to battle a myriad of injuries as his body breaks down. He had back, hamstring, and arm issues all in 2024. The 43 innings he threw resulted in 40 Ks, a 3.95 ERA, and a 1.15 WHIP. So, Scherzer is still useful when he takes the mound, but the amount of time he takes the mound is not enough for him to be useful in fantasy.

18. **Ronel Blanco, HOU:** One of the "feel good" stories of last season, Blanco threw a no-hitter and became relevant out of nowhere in his age 30 season after being out of baseball. That doesn't mean I'm buying the vibes in 2025. His 2.80 ERA is not the full story. The xERA (3.97), FIP (4.15), and xFIP (4.42) all scream regression. Sometimes, when a story is too good to be true, that's because it is.

19. **Jesus Luzardo, PHI:** After teasing us in 2023, Luzardo once again dropped a flaming bag of poop on our doorsteps in 2024. Luzardo suffered a 5.00 ERA over 66.2 innings before a lumbar stress reaction mercifully ended his season. His K/9 dropped from 10.48 to 7.83, and Luzardo never stabilized. It's hard to believe he's just 28 years old, and I don't think he's "done," but I'd rather let someone else gamble on Luzardo in 2025. Although, the move to Philly does peak my interest at an extreme discount.

20. **Bobby Miller, LAD:** Ah, the curious case of Bobby Miller. What appeared to be a great draft day value in 2024 was anything but that. An 8.52 ERA and a 1.77 WHIP over 56 innings leave us wondering if he was ever healthy. Will he ever regain his promise? Hopefully, he will turn things around, but after last season, fantasy managers will need a lot of convincing.

21. **Aaron Civale, MIL:** After 17 games with the Rays and a 5 ERA, Civale was dealt to the Brewers, and his ERA plummeted to 3.53. However, his FIP in both spots was 4.79. Now, maybe the Brewers did make some adjustments we can believe in, considering he went 6-1 with a 2.57 ERA over his final nine starts. But Civale has been a league-average pitcher most of his career, so be careful when buying too much into a good run.

22. **Andrew Abbott, CIN:** A shoulder injury that cut his 2024 season short makes his '25 prospects cloudy. Not to mention, his 5.04 FIP and 1.29 WHIP are not the stuff good pitching seasons are made of, so it may be best to steer clear of him, regardless of cost or Spring outlook.

23. **Javier Assad, CHC:** Assad seemingly came out of nowhere last season, and on the surface, his 3.73 ERA seems respectable. Unfortunately, he had a 4.97 xERA lurking below and a 5.82 ERA over his last six starts with a 1.43 WHIP. It was clear the league adjusted, and he couldn't respond in turn. Assad's 2025 value is in question.

24. **Frankie Montas, NYM:** Montas was incredibly inconsistent from start to start, and it's fair to assume he may never regain his peak Oakland form. With an ERA approaching 5 and a 1.37 WHIP, it's best to avoid Montas in 2025. The Mets did resurrect the careers of Sean Manaea and Luis Severino, so it's not impossible he's the next "project" that succeeds. That success is far from a lock.

25. **Eduardo Rodriguez, ARI:** Man, I had high hopes for Rodriguez last year after a fantastic 2023 season, but injuries crushed his 2024 season and now leave him as a late-round flier at best heading into '25. He's only 31, so there's still time to right the ship. There's no denying last year was a 5 ERA disaster.

26. **Clayton Kershaw, LAD:** Kershaw says he's coming back in 2025, but he'll be 37 and coming off a 4.50 ERA and 1.50 WHIP over 30 innings in 2024. There are better uses of your draft capital.

27. **Miles Mikolas, STL:** Mikolas is turning 37 and had a 5.35 ERA, 1.28 WHIP, and 122 K/25 BB over 32 starts. Hard pass.

28. **Tyler Anderson, LAA:** Anderson's 2024 season was the definition of smoke and mirrors. His 3.81 ERA over 179 innings was a miracle when you consider his xERA was 4.37, his FIP was 4.66, and his xFIP was 4.85. He has a below-average strikeout rate and a walk rate that is too high. What are you doing drafting him?

29. **Jon Gray, TEX:** Jon Gray seems forever snakebit, which is a shame because he's shown some signs of life after escaping Colorado. Alas, Gray only made 19 starts (a foot injury this time ended his season) and was mediocre over those innings. At 33, time is running out for him ever to realize his potential.

30. **Braxton Garrett, MIA:** Garrett suffered a strained forearm and then an elbow impingement during rehab. His 5.35 ERA certainly showed he was not right before the IL stint, but he has a long way to go before he proves he's healthy enough to be an asset in 2025. Investing in pitchers with existing arm troubles is not sound practice.

31. **Lance Lynn, FA:** The body seems to be betraying Lynn and a knee issue cost him the end of 2024. He still has some strikeout potential, but 38, the sun is setting on his fantasy value. The 4.93 xERA is troubling.

32. **Marcus Stroman, NYY:** A 1.47 WHIP and a 4.31 ERA with a woeful K rate is a bad investment.

33. **Taijuan Walker, PHI:** A 7.10 and a 1.72 WHIP. No! Stop drafting him!

34. **Griffin Canning, NYM:** Too many hits and not enough strikeouts make Griffin a bad fantasy investment. Although, the Mets seem to have a touch with "project guys".

35. **Patrick Sandoval, LAA:** The same goes for Sandoval.

36. **Edward Cabrera, MIA**: He offers strikeout potential and occasionally teases with a good performance, but his 4.95 ERA and 1.37 WHIP are too much to bear.

37. **Ben Lively, CLE:** Lively made 29 starts, but his strikeout rate is too low to be appealing. In leagues where you get points for innings, he can be rostered, but his xFIP and FIP are well above 4.50, which screams to stay away.

38. **Chris Paddack, MIN:** A two-pitch pitcher who will give you hope and then crush your dreams with his 4.99 ERA. Stay away. Far too hittable.

39. **Luis Ortiz, CLE:** Ratios are mid, K rate is low, walk rate is too high, and deeper stats suggest regression. Maybe Cleveland can fix him.

40. **Keider Montero, DET:** Montero is just 24 years old with strikeout potential, but his minor league track record doesn't impress, nor did his time with the big club

41. **Reid Detmers, LAA:** Detmers once upon a time carried some mild intrigue, but his 6.70 ERA should cure you of any further curiosities.

42. **Bailey Falter, PIT:** Not nearly enough strikeout appeal.

43. **Colorado Pitchers, COL:** Just don't. They will kill your rotation.

Up and Coming

1. **MacKenzie Gore, WAS:** Gore had a great 9.7 K/9 last year, and his 3.90 ERA is just pushing the limit of tolerable. Gore is just turning 26 (it feels like he's been around forever), and his September finish (1.28 ERA/.82 WHIP over five starts) gives me hope for 2025. There's a quietly good trend happening here. In a world where "sleepers" don't really exist, Gore may actually be one based on his profile and cost.

2. **Ryan Weathers, MIA**: One of the lone bright spots for the Marlins was Weathers in 2024. He made 16 starts with a 3.63 ERA, 1.18 WHIP, with a strong K/BB rate. Now, his xERA and FIP were 4.11, so expect some regression in 2025 and wins to be scarce, but Weathers has the pedigree to become a solid fantasy starter as early as next year.

3. **Bowden Francis, TOR:** Francis showed some promise and a quality start streak towards the season's end. The new splitter moved him into the rotation, where he posted a 1.80 ERA, 0.60 WHIP, and 58 K/8 BB in 65 IP. He will probably be a deep sleeper on a lot of boards, and I would agree with that, considering that the Jays' rotation is going to yield him opportunities once again.

4. **Cade Povich, BAL:** Cade Povich was rushed a bit to the big leagues after injuries befell the O's rotation. There were struggles but also improvements. In September starts, Povich posted a 2.60 ERA, 0.87 WHIP, and 32 K/8 BB over 27.2 innings. There are some similarities to Taj Bradley year over year. Another top pitching prospect rushed too soon but starts figuring it out. Povich should be on your 2025 radar.

5. **Ryan Pepiot, TB:** His versatility may work against him in 2025. Ryan Pepiot certainly deserves another shot at the rotation, but with returning top guys, he could be squeezed into the bullpen. Pepiot looked like a nice return for Tyler Glasnow, pitching to a 3.60 ERA, 1.15 WHIP, and 142 K/48 BB in 130 innings over 26 starts.

6. **Shane Baz, TB:** Tampa is filled with pitching promise, and Shane Baz showed upside across 14 starts last season with the big club. He posted a 3.06 ERA, 1.06 WHIP, and a 69 K/27 BB ratio over 79.1 IP. A great sign of recovery from Tommy John, Baz seems primed to reach 150 innings in 2025. However, there is a lot of competition in this rotation, so he needs to have a strong Spring to hold his spot. At 26, Baz looks like a future front-of-the-rotation starter, but I think that could be at least a season or more away from coming to fruition.

7. **D.J. Herz, WAS:** The 23-year-old Herz got a shot at the Nats rotation and showed some promise. Over 19 starts, Herz had a 1.26 WHIP and a 4.16 ERA. His xERA (3.29), FIP (3.71), and xFIP (3.85) were all better than that ERA number, suggesting the best is yet to come in 2025. He carries an elite 10 K/9, and his 3.67 ERA over 320 minor-league innings is very encouraging. He's a 2025 sleeper.

8. **Tobias Myers, MIL:** Meyers was a surprising positive for the Brewers rotation. He made 25 starts, posted a 3.00 ERA and a 1.17 WHIP. Now, the deeper numbers suggest an ERA closer to 4 is on the horizon, and his minor league track record confirms that likelihood. At 26, he has development to come and could be a useful depth piece in '25.

9. **Jose Butto, NYM:** The Mets rotation for 2025 will be in assembly mode this off-season, but Butto had some moments for the Mets. His 4 BB/9 is not a good look, but his 10 K/9 at 26 years old is exciting. He was very tough to square up and hit, but too many baserunners led to inefficiency at times. There's upside here, as indicated by his 2.55 ERA and 1.07 WHIP over 74 major league innings. However, that 6.47 FIP is a reminder he could blow up in a bad way if he doesn't get that control under wraps.

10. **Drew Thorpe, CWS:** Thorpe was dominant in the minors last year at AA with a 1.35 ERA over 11 starts. Unfortunately, he plays for the dysfunctional White Sox, who rushed him to the big leagues, and he got crushed to a 5.89 ERA over his nine big league starts. The 24-year-old Thorpe has a ton of potential, but my faith in the White Sox to develop him properly is low, to say the least. His long-term outlook is better than his 2025 value.

11. **Louie Varland, MIN:** Varland is at a fork in the road where he has nothing left to prove in the minors (3.33 ERA over 80 minor league games) but can't seem to make the transition to the majors (5.51 career ERA). At 27, this is the pitch or get-off-the-pot scenario for Varland as he angles for a spot in the Twins 2025 rotation. He's more of a waiver wire add for me than a draft with the exception of deep leagues and AL-only scenarios.

12. **Max Meyer, MIA:** Injuries and the Marlins front office are dangerously close to killing a bright young career when it comes to Max Meyer. After a nice start to the season, he was sent down for "innings limits" (as if the Marlins were worried about October; insert eye roll here). He was a four-inning starter there and then eventually made his way back but struggled to a 5.68 ERA. He's shown in the minor leagues that he has some serious potential, and at 26, there's still time to realize it.

Serviceable

1. **Zach Eflin, BAL:** Eflin was dealt to the Orioles and showed some improvement. After 19 starts with the Rays and a 4.09 ERA, in his nine starts with Baltimore, that ERA was 2.60. The good news is he doesn't walk anyone. The bad news is he doesn't really strike out a lot either (career 7.8 K/9). He's an innings eater with decent peripherals.

2. **Brayan Bello, BOS:** The 25-year-old Bello made 30 starts for the Red Sox last year and delivered a 14-6 record despite a 4.46 ERA and a 1.36 WHIP. His K/9 rate is average, but his 3.5 BB/9 is not ideal. That 4.81 ERA at home needs a lot of work, too! His 3.87 xFIP gives you a tiny bit of hope for improvement. Bello is a part of the Sox rotation future, but right now, he looks to be more filler than front liner, at least for now.

3. **Luis Severino, ATH:** Severino got his career back on track last season, throwing 182 innings over 31 starts. His 3.91 was ok, but his 4.21 FIP is a more likely 2025 outcome. If he can keep that BB/9 under 3 again, he should be a decent back-end rotation piece in fantasy. His 5.02 road ERA versus 2.97 home mark is worrisome, and his monthly ERA was very up and down overall. Still, Severino is only 31, so he should, at the very least, be a 30-start guy with a low 4 ERA, which is useful in mixed leagues when he's on a good streak. The hurdle is playing for the Athletics in a minor league stadium.

4. **Jameson Taillon, CHC:** Taillon won 12 games over 28 starts with a 3.27 ERA, a 1.13 WHIP, and 125 K/33 BB over 165 IP. All the underlying metrics suggest his ERA should have been closer to 4, but Taillon remains a decent roto rotation depth guy despite a lower-than-ideal strikeout rate. If the K rate rebounds in 2025, he could maintain his '24 success.

5. **Jordan Montgomery, ARI**: Montgomery had established himself as a solid major league pitcher. But then, a late signing this off-season set back his routine, and he never recuperated the way Blake Snell eventually did. He ended up with a 6.23 ERA and a 1.65 WHIP over 117 innings (but deep numbers suggest that ERA should have been more like 4.75). It was a bad marriage. I absolutely think a new environment and regular routine will see him get back to being a mid-3 ERA, back-end fantasy rotation guy.

6. **Ryne Nelson, ARI:** Nelson went 10-6 with a 4.24 ERA and a 1.25 WHIP. He's a league-average pitcher with a 4:1 K/BB ratio, which makes one hopeful he can build on that and eventually achieve more—a decent back-end/depth arm in 2025, at minimum.

7. **Tylor Megill, NYM:** Megill's 4 ERA and 1.31 ERA are nothing special, but his 10.5 K/9 rate is very intriguing. His 3.55 FIP and 3.79 xFIP suggest that if he's finally given a full season, he could become a fantasy asset very quickly. Also of note is his 2.76 ERA, 1.02 WHIP, and 28 K/ 9 BB across 29.1 innings in the second half. He's 29, so it may be now or never for him to reach his potential.

8. **David Peterson, NYM:** The lefty turns 30 this season and is on the precipice of harnessing his potential. Over 21 starts, Peterson had a 2.90 ERA and a 1.29 WHIP. But his xERA and xFIP suggest that ERA could rise closer to 4 in 2025. His K/9 dropped, but so did his walk rate. If the K/9 gets back to 9 at least and the walk rate remains low, then Peterson could be in line for that classic "late blooming lefty" season.

9. **Kyle Harrison, SF:** Harrison took some lumps in his first real rotation run and missed the end of the year with shoulder inflammation after 124 innings. Health must be monitored, but you saw glimpses of Harrison's talent. It's about consistency and health if he's going to take a step forward in 2025.

10. **Mathew Boyd, CHC:** Boyd returned from elbow surgery and turned in a useful 2.72 ERA and 1.13 WHIP over eight starts. He'll be 34 next year and has been largely an enigma throughout his career. Perhaps better health and whatever the Cleveland coaching staff tweaked could give us hope for a decent '25. The 10.4 K/9 over his 39 IPs are encouraging.

11. **Jordan Hicks, SF:** Hicks's season went almost exactly as I planned it; a good start, followed by fading, inning limits, move to pen, and eventual shoulder soreness due to workload. He simply ran out of gas. Now, the hope is that rest and experience will make him a candidate to become more reliable for a longer stretch in 2025, but there are no guarantees there.

12. **Reese Olson, DET:** Although inconsistent at times, Olson delivered a 3.53 ERA and a 1.18 WHIP over 26 starts. Cutting his HR allowed by half was a big reason for his year-over-year progress. He turns 25 this year and looks like a decent, deep-league bench arm based on his 3.17 FIP.

13. **Spencer Turnbull, FA:** Turnbull earned a rotation opportunity and over 7 starts and 54 innings he had a strong 2.65 ERA and 1.05 WHIP. Then a lat injury robbed us of most of his 2024. Turnbull is one of the more interesting late round fliers based on his age (32) and 2024 moments. A dart worth throwing for free depending on his rotation opportunity.

14. **Dean Kremer, BAL:** You like the 3 to 1 K/BB ratio, but the 4.10 ERA screams league-average starter. It was encouraging that he finished strong after a slump in the summer.

15. **Chris Bassitt, TOR:** This ten-year veteran is nearing the twilight years. He gave you 170 innings last year, but it came with a 4.16 ERA and a gross 1.46 WHIP. I'm confident this version of Bassitt is what awaits you in 2025. He'll take the ball every fifth day, and you'll hold your breath.

16. **Jose Quintana, FA:** The 35-year-old Quintana made some big starts for the Mets down the stretch, but from a fantasy perspective, his sub-par K rate doesn't make him a great investment. His 3.75 ERA and 1.25 WHIP were good enough to be a .500 pitcher, and he should be good for 170 innings again in '25. He's a better "real-life" pitcher than a fantasy asset.

17. **Andrew Heaney, FA:** Heaney didn't deserve to lose 14 games, but he didn't deserve to win 14 either. Heaney is a low 4 ERA pitcher with a 3:1 K/BB ratio. He had an ERA over 6 in April and in September, but everything in between was decent. But it's those annual bad stretches that always hold him back.

18. **Spencer Arrighetti, HOU:** 2024 was a roller coaster for Arrighetti, but he did provide a lot of strikeouts (171 in 145 IP). The trouble was his 4 BB/9 that inflated his WHIP to a crazy 1.41. That won't cut it in roto leagues, but in points leagues, if he can improve that in '25, his strikeouts are intriguing. The good news is that the deeper stats suggest his ERA should be closer to 4 flat and that makes him worthy of a bench look.

19. **Jake Irvin, WAS:** The Nationals are a team on the upswing, and Jake Irving did go 187 innings in '24. He has a 3:1 K/BB ratio but a below-average K rate. He still has his prime ahead of him and could make some headway in 2025. He doesn't have an elite pedigree, but he could become a solid back-of-the-rotation starter in the years to come.

20. **Andre Pallante, STL:** With so much of last year's Cardinals rotation aging up and out of usefulness, Pallante has a chance to pay some dividends. The 26-year-old Pallante finished the season with a 2.98 ERA over his last nine starts, and his overall 3.78 ERA and 1.30 WHIP in 121 innings this season were useful.

Streamers - AL/NL Only

1. **Tyler Mahle, TEX:** He returned from injury late in the year but, of course, didn't look sharp. He has some valuable strikeout potential if he is truly healthy in 2025.

2. **Landon Knack, LAD:** He had some moments for the Dodgers, but the league caught up quickly. His shot at a rotation spot is dicey in 2025. More of a depth arm if you already have multiple Dodgers starters on your roster.

3. **Gavin Williams, CLE:** Williams was not quite ready for prime time, with a 4.86 ERA over 76 big league innings. The upside is still there, but he's more of a late flier or AL-only option.

4. **Jose Soriano, LAA:** Over 20 starts, Soriano returned a modest 3.42 ERA and a 1.20 WHIP despite a lower-than-ideal K/9. He's a depth piece who is pitching on a bad team.

5. **Mitchell Parker, WAS:** Parker had an 11 K/9 in the minors, but that rate didn't transfer to the big leagues last year for the 24-year-old. His sputtered out after the break to a 4.79 ERA, but his first 11 starts were solid enough to warrant deeper league interest.

6. **Kyle Gibson, FA:** He turns 38 and has been painfully "mid" for most of his career. He's a waiver wire band-aid at best this season.

7. **Matt Waldron, SD:** Knuckleballers usually have a few good runs in them, but sustainability is an issue, hence the 4.91 ERA.

8. **J.P. Sears, A's:** Sears is an innings eater in a weird environment. No mixed-league appeal here.

9. **Martin Perez, FA:** Annual waiver wire rotation band-aid.

10. **Colin Rea, MIL:** Rea won 12 games despite a below-average strikeout rate—a journeyman with little fantasy value.

11. **Simeon Woods Richardson, MIN:** He threw 133 innings over 28 starts for the Twins with a below-average strikeout rate and a pedestrian 4.17 ERA and 1.29 WHIP. He's young enough to improve those stats, but his minor-league stats support mediocrity.

12. **Casey Mize, DET:** Mize is now 27, so the clock is ticking for him to realize his once high-end prospect status. His 4.49 ERA and 1.47 WHIP were not good enough to make you optimistic about 2025.

13. **Alex Cobb, DET:** At 37, Cobb is, at best, a deep-league bench guy who could make a few starts in a pinch for you.

See You in 2026

1. **Joe Musgrove, SD:** This was inevitable and a shame since Musgrove had been battling injuries already. At his best, he's a dominant strikeout guy. Buy low in dynasty and hope for a healthy recovery.

2. **Gavin Stone, LAD:** Did you know Gavin Stone led the Dodgers in starts last year? Unfortunately, Stone underwent right shoulder surgery and will miss the entire 2025 season.

3. **Kyle Bradish, BAL:** After a dreadful April of 2023, Bradish took off, but unfortunately the arm gave out. Plenty of hope left he can come back and get right in 2026.

4. **Cristian Javier, HOU:** Electric arm, needs better secondary stuff and could end up a closer at some point.

5. **Jose Urquidy, HOU:** An innings eater who won't be eating any in 2025.

6. **Christian Scott, NYM:** A bright future, I'd be buying and he will be in the Mets rotation by mid-2026.

7. **John Means, FA:** I think we are in the twilight here.

8. **Alek Manoah, TOR:** This roller coaster will make you sick. Run away.

9. **Ricky Tiedemann, TOR:** It is starting to feel like too much time lost in development.

10. **Emmet Sheehan, LAD:** Intriguing dynasty stash.

Chapter 4

Relief Pitchers

	Shallow League RP	RPV
1	Emmanuel Clase	22%
2	Devin Williams	3%
3	Mason Miller	2%
4	Josh Hader	7%
5	Ryan Helsley	7%
6	Raisel Iglesias	5%
7	Edwin Diaz	3%
8	Felix Bautista	3%
9	Robert Suarez	3%
10	Jhoan Duran	2%
11	Andres Munoz	2%
12	Ryan Walker	-8%
13	Lucas Erceg	-10%
14	Kirby Yates	-10%
15	Alexis Diaz	-15%
16	Pete Fairbanks	-15%

	Deep League RPV	RPV
1	Emmanuel Clase	33%
2	Devin Williams	13%
3	Mason Miller	11%
4	Josh Hader	16%
5	Ryan Helsley	16%
6	Raisel Iglesias	15%
7	Edwin Diaz	13%
8	Felix Bautista	13%
9	Robert Suarez	13%
10	Jhoan Duran	11%
11	Andres Munoz	11%
12	Ryan Walker	0%
13	Lucas Erceg	-2%
14	Kirby Yates	-2%
15	Alexis Diaz	-8%
16	Pete Fairbanks	-8%
17	Kyle Finnegan	-9%
18	Ben Joyce	-9%
19	Trevor Megill	-13%
20	Jordan Romano	-17%
21	David Bednar	-17%
22	Tanner Scott	-26%
23	Carlos Estevez	-26%
24	Aroldis Chapman	-26%

*** Get updated RPV Cheat for one time $5 cost (free updates)
PayPal: FantasyBlackBook@gmail.com or Venmo: @FantasyBlackBook
And include your email address ***

Relief Pitcher Profiles and Overview

By Brian Entrekin

There are many philosophies about drafting relievers. Some like to take two top-end relievers early, some take one and wait, and others just play the waiting game and do not mind finding saves on the waiver wire. All of these angles can result in success; it just depends on your comfort level when it comes to saves.

When looking back at the relief pitching position for the 2024 season, we saw two closers collect over 40 saves and at least 30 saves by eight pitchers. If you decided to wait, you may be in luck, as there were 22 pitchers with at least 20 saves. It gets better if you like the waiver wire, as there were 39 pitchers with at least ten saves and 222 pitchers recorded at least one save.

Looking ahead at the 2025 season, the position has 12-14 closers who seemed locked into a solid closing role. There are also nearly ten free-agent relievers that could bring in a solid amount of saves. No matter how you approach the position on draft day, there are plenty of options on the draft board.

The Elite

1. **Emmanuel Clase, CLE (G: 74 | 47 SV):** Clase is coming off an outstanding season closing for the Guardians. It was his third straight season with at least 42 saves and his fourth straight season with at least 71 appearances. That's some excellent consistency when drafting a closer. After a down ratio season in 2023, Clase bounced back significantly with an ERA of 0.61 and 0.66 WHIP. Clase also rebounded to a 20.7% K-BB after a dismal 15.9% K-BB in 2023, giving him a K-BB over 20% in three of the last four years. Barring an injury, Clase is THE elite closer in the game, with some of the best consistency in baseball.

2. **Devin Williams, NYY (G: 22 | 14 SV):** Williams missed the first four months of the season after suffering a stress fracture in his back during spring training. Once he returned, he immediately returned to the closing role for the Brewers. He made 22 appearances, collecting 14 saves and a win over 21.2 innings pitched. Williams was great yet again, with a 1.25 ERA, 0.97 WHIP, and an insane 43.2% strikeout rate. It was Williams's third season with an ERA in the 1s and his third straight year with a WHIP of 1.01 or less. He racked up a 30.7% K-BB, which was the best of his career as he returned to dominance. Williams is now the closer for the Yankees so opportunities will be abundant. It's all how he handles the big city lights.

3. **Josh Hader, HOU (G: 71 | 34 SV):** Hader once again racked up the saves but was a wild card in the ratio department. Hader collected 34 saves, giving him 33 or more saves over the last five non-covid seasons. Conversely, the ratios took a step back, as he had a 3.80 ERA after a 1.28 ERA in 2023. Hader's last four seasons have seen an ERA of 3.80, 1.28, 5.22, and 1.23. The jump in ERA has correlated with massive spikes in HR/FB, which leaves hope that Hader can return to a low ERA arm. The ERA is the only real issue with Hader as he's consistent in saves, strikeouts with a rate of 36% or better each year since 2017, and WHIP with a WHIP below one in five of seven seasons. Hader is great, and closing on a great team makes him an elite option.

4. **Raisel Iglesias, ATL (G: 66 | 34 SV):** When looking for an elite closer, consistency is king, and Iglesias has been one of the more consistent closers for years. Since 2017, Iglesias has had 28 or more saves in six of eight seasons, only missing in 2020 (COVID) and 2022, when he was traded to be a setup man in Atlanta. Since 2016, Iglesias has had an ERA of 2.75 or better in eight years, with a WHIP of 1.22 or lower in all nine years. But wait, there's more, as Iglesias has a K-BB of 21.2% or better in each of the last six seasons and seven of the previous eight. Iglesias has quietly been elite and deserves to be in the conversation with the last three closers.

Top Talent

1. **Mason Miller, ATH (G: 55 |28 SV):** Miller was outstanding in his first season as a closer for the A's. He finished the season with 28 saves in 55 appearances over 65 innings pitched. He collected an excellent 2.49 ERA with a 1.91 SIERA and .88 WHIP. Miller had an elite 41.8% strikeout rate supported by a 19.6% SwStr and was part of an elite 33.3% K-BB. Miller is a top talent with elite upside. His team is the only thing holding him back, which could limit his total saves.

2. **Felix Bautista, BAL (G: 0 | 0 SV):** Bautista missed the entire 2024 season recovering from Tommy John surgery, and he'll look to return to a top-end closer in 2025. In 2023, Bautista was elite with 33 saves and eight wins in 56 appearances. He dominated with a 1.48 ERA and 0.92 WHIP with an elite 46.4% strikeout rate and 35.4% K-BB. Bautista has had a WHIP below 1.00 in his first two seasons, with an ERA of 2.19 or better and a K-BB of 25% or better. Bautista has been great, and he should be well recovered from surgery heading into 2025.

3. **Robert Suarez, SD (G: 65 | 36 SV):** Suarez was outstanding in his first season in the closing role. He collected nine wins and 36 saves over 65 appearances. Suarez collected a solid 2.77 ERA and 1.05 WHIP. He dominated but did not bring the elite strikeout upside other top talent closers showcase. This past year, Suarez had a 22.9% strikeout rate and 16.7% K-BB. There are rumors that San Diego could trade Suarez this season, but for now, he is locked in as the Padres closer, which is a great team to close for regarding fantasy.

4. **Edwin Diaz, NYM (G: 54 G | 20 SV):** After missing 2023 with a knee injury, Diaz had a 2024 season with mixed results. He collected 20 saves and six wins. That's not bad, but Diaz also blew seven saves to go with a 3.52 ERA. The blown saves are not ideal, but the skills were still strong, with a 38.9% strikeout rate, 17.3% SwStr, and 29.6% K-BB. Diaz can be elite, but he doesn't kill you when he struggles, which still results in a top fantasy talent.

5. **Ryan Helsley, STL (G: 65 G | 49 SV):** After a couple of seasons of sharing closing roles in St. Louis, Helsley erupted in 2024. He led MLB with 49 saves while collecting seven wins in 65 innings pitched. He had a 2.04 ERA and 1.10 WHIP, his third straight season with an ERA of 2.45 or less and a WHIP of 1.10 or less. It was Helsey's third consecutive season with a K-BB of 21.1% or better and a 16% SwStr or better. His skills have been solid, and they all came to fruition during a monster season. It's a season that will be tough to duplicate regarding saves, but it should still be good for 30+ saves, which we'll take all day.

Solid Options

1. **Jhoan Duran, MIN (G: 58 | 23 SV):** Duran has showcased electric stuff in his career but has yet to put together an elite season as a closer. In 2024, Duran had a 3.64 ERA, 2.50 SIERA and 1.16 WHIP. He has not saved more than 27 games in a season, with an ERA of 2.45 or higher each season. Again, the stuff is great, with a strikeout rate of over 29% each season with a K-BB of 22.4% or higher. Duran may put together a monster season someday, but there are limitations with usage in Minnesota and overall skills.

2. **Andrés Munoz, SEA (G: 60 | 22 SV):** Munoz took over closing duties for the Mariners in 2024 and was dominant. He collected 22 saves over 60 appearances with a 2.12 ERA, 0.96 WHIP, and 22% K-BB. Munoz should step back into the closing role in Seattle for 2025, and he has the skills to provide 30+ saves with elite strikeout upside.

3. **Lucas Erceg, KC (G: 61 | 14 SV):** Erceg has been a strong reliever in the past and was finally able to showcase those skills in a closing role in 2024. He was traded to the Royals at the trade deadline and became a dominant closer. In 23 appearances with the Royals, Erceg collected 11 saves with six holds. He struck out 31 over 25 innings pitched with a 28.9% K-BB. Erceg was lights out and has the skills to dominate the ninth for the Royals again in 2025.

Red Flags

1. **David Bednar, PIT (G: 62 | 23 SV):** Bednar collected 23 saves this season, but that's the only good thing from him in 2024. He had a 5.77 ERA and 1.42 WHIP before losing his job to Aroldis Chapman. Bednar is penciled in as the Pirates' closer, but it is not a safe situation, as one free agent signing is all the Pirates need to demote him yet again.

2. **Pete Fairbanks, TB (G: 46 | 23 SV):** Fairbanks collected 23 saves in 2024 after 25 saves in 2023, but some concerns surround Fairbanks. He had an ERA of 3.57 after a 2.58 ERA in 2023. His walk rate rose to 9.2%, close to the 10% or higher that he had in five of six seasons—the high walk rate, with a career-low 23.8%, correlated to a bad 14.6% K-BB. Fairbanks's injury history and diminished skills make for a very concerning situation when drafting a closer.

3. **Jordan Romano, FA (G: 15 | 8 SV):** Romano only tallied 13.2 innings in 2024 due to a shoulder injury from which he never returned. Shoulder injuries are already concerning enough, but Romano was also non-tendered by the Jays, making Romano a free agent. The fact that the Jays let Romano go makes one think Romano may not be fully healthy. It makes sense to steer clear of Romano this season.

Serviceable

1. **Luke Weaver, NYY (G: 62 G | 4 SV):** Weaver never made it as a starter, but this past season, he found his way in the back end of the Yankees' bullpen. He became a lights-out closer late in the season and into the postseason. The metrics look great, too, as Weaver had a 31.1% strikeout rate, 15.4% SwStr, and 23.3% K-BB. He will again be a part of the backend of the Yankees' bullpen and should get the first crack at the closing duties if Williams picks up an injury.

2. **Ryan Walker, SF (G: 76 | 10 SV):** Walker was one of the better relievers in baseball last season, and once Camilo Doval failed as the Giants' closer, he flourished in that role as well. Walker appeared in 76 games, collecting ten wins and ten saves with a 1.91 ERA and 0.85 WHIP. Walker even struck out 32.1% of the batters he faced for a 26.3% K-BB. He was outstanding; a huge 2025 could be in store for the Giants closer.

3. **Michael Kopech, LAD (G: 67 | 15 SV):** Kopech started the season as the White Sox closer but struggled with control and consistency. He was traded to the Dodgers and looked like a brand-new man. Over 24 appearances with the Dodgers, Kopech collected four wins, eight holds, and six saves. He had an outstanding 1.13 ERA with a 33% strikeout rate and 21.6% K-BB. Kopech still had some control issues with an 11.4% walk rate, and now could miss the opening of the season with an injury.

4. **Alexis Diaz, CIN (G: 60 | 28 SV):** Diaz brings major ratio concerns as a closer with a 3.99 ERA this past season and a 1.30 WHIP. His strikeout rate dropped this past season to 22.7% from over 30% in his previous seasons. Even with the lackluster ratios, Diaz has collected 28 and 37 saves in the last two years, which makes him an attractive closing option later in drafts.

5. **Porter Hodge, CHC (G: 39 G | 9 SV):** In his first season in the bigs, Hodge took over closing duties for the Cubs late in the season and collected nine saves. He had a strong 1.88 ERA and 0.88 WHIP with a 31.7% strikeout rate. Hodge has showcased great strikeout rates throughout the minors, with a bit too many walks as well. He should get the first crack at closer for the Cubs.

6. **Calvin Faucher, MIA (G: 53 | 6 SV):** After the Marlins traded Tanner Scott to the Padres, Faucher took over closing duties to collect six saves. Over his 53.2 innings, he had a 3.19 ERA and 1.40 WHIP. The ratios could be better, but he should be the closer for the Marlins, which has plenty of fantasy viability, as we saw with Scott before he was traded.

Question Marks

1. **A.J. Puk, ARI (G: 62 | 3 SV):** Puk had a tale of two seasons. He started in Miami as the closer, struggled, lost his job, and was traded to the DBacks. In Arizona, Puk found his former self and was quite solid. In 30 appearances with the DBacks, Puk had a 1.32 ERA with an elite 41.7% strikeout rate and 36.9% K-BB. He picked up seven holds and two saves as well. Puk could be a solid closer for the DBacks, but Justin Martinez will also receive a chance at saves in Arizona.

2. **Ben Joyce, LAA (G: 31 | 4 SV):** After the Angels traded Carlos Estevez to the Phillies, Joyce became one of a few options for saves in the Angels bullpen. He finished the season with four saves in 31 appearances with a 2.08 ERA and 1.15 WHIP. He should open the season as the Angels closer, but he needs to work on his command to keep the job all season.

3. **Liam Hendriks, BOS (G: 0 | 0 SV):** After being one of the best closers in baseball in 2021 and 2022, Hendriks needed Tommy John surgery in early 2023 and missed 2024. He's reportedly healthy and ready to take over closing duties in Boston.

4. **Orion Kerkering, PHI (G: 64 | 0 SV):** The Phillies had plenty of hands in the same cookie jar in 2024, but many options are no longer in Philadelphia. Kerkering did not receive a save in 2024 but was one of the Phillies' best closers and could be in line to take over closing duties in 2025. The primary question depends on whether the Phillies sign a closer and push Kerkering back to the 8th inning.

5. **Beau Brieske, DET (G: 46 G | 1 SV):** Similar to Philadelphia, there were a lot of relievers getting saves in Detroit. Brieske did not receive a single save in the regular season but was a significant piece in the late innings during the playoffs. Will Vest, Jason Foley, and Tyler Holton can also factor into saves in Detroit.

Wild Cards

1. **Kirby Yates, LAD (G: 61 | 33 SV):** After years of injuries, Yates returned to a closing role with the Rangers and collected 33 saves with a 1.17 ERA and 0.83 WHIP. With Michael Kopech on the shelf, Yates has a shot at the closer role.

2. **Tanner Scott, LAD (G: 72 | 22 SV):** Scott recorded 22 saves between the Marlins and Padres last season. He has recorded 20 or more saves in two of the previous three years. Like Yates, Scott could also see early save opportunities in LA.

3. **Kyle Finnegan, WAS (G: 65 | 38 SV):** Finnegan has recorded 66 saves over the last two saves for the Nats, yet the Nats non-tendered Finnegan after the 2024 season. He would be a solid closer if signed to a team in need.

4. **Blake Treinen, LAD (G: 50 | 1 SV):** Treinen was a solid late-inning arm for the Dodgers last season and even served in the closing role on their World Series run. Expect a similar season now that he returned to LA.

5. **Aroldis Chapman, BOS (G: 68 | 14 G):** Chapman was one of the best closers in baseball for years but eventually lost control on the mound. That changed last year with the Pirates as he collected 14 saves after taking over for David Bednar. Chapman should get first crack at saves in Boston.

6. **Kenley Jansen, FA (G: 54 | 27 SV):** Jansen has saved 25 or more saves in the last 12 non-Covid seasons. He's getting older, and the dominance is not what it once was, but the saves continue to rack up when Jansen is on the mound.

7. **Carlos Estevez, FA (G: 54 | 26 SV):** Estevez has collected 57 saves over the last two seasons, yet no team is willing to keep him. He will likely be a cheap closing free agent for some team and a cheap fantasy draft pick as well.

8. **Clay Holmes, NYM (G: 67 | 30 SV):** Holmes has collected 20 or more saves in the last three seasons. The Mets are considering him for the rotation in 2025. Could he be the next Seth Lugo? Perhaps. Or just a setup man for Diaz.

9. **Tyler Kinley, COL (G: 67 | 12 SV):** Kinley picked up 12 saves with the Rockies last season, but that came with a 6.19 ERA and 1.47 WHIP. There is a lot of risk with drafting Kinley, but for now, he appears to be the closer for the Rockies.

And finally, we are left with a handful of relievers who would benefit immensely from the inherited closer struggling or, worse, an injury. They may also contribute to your fantasy ratios, steal wins in relief, and increase your team strikeout numbers.

- **Trevor Megill, MIL (G: 48 G | 21 SV)**
- **Jason Adam, SD (G: 74 | 4 SV)**
- **Evan Phillips, LAD (G: 61 | 18 G)**
- **Cade Smith, CLE (G: 74 G | 1 SV)**
- **Ian Hamilton, NYY (G: 35 | 1 SV)**
- **Edwin Uceta, MIA (G: 30 | 5 SV)**

Chapter 5

Catchers

	Single Catcher Formats	RPV
1	William Contreras	40%
2	Adley Rutschman	19%
3	Yainer Diaz	16%
4	Cal Raleigh	12%
5	Will Smith	5%
6	Salvador Perez	-2%
7	Shea Langeliers	-2%
8	Logan O'Hoppe	-3%
9	Francisco Alvarez	-3%
10	Willson Contreras	-3%
11	Tyler Stephenson	-5%
12	J.T. Realmuto	-10%
13	Ryan Jeffers	-15%
14	Sean Murphy	-16%
15	Austin Wells	-16%
16	Conor Wong	-16%

	2 Catcher Formats	RPV
1	William Contreras	55%
2	Adley Rutschman	32%
3	Yainer Diaz	29%
4	Cal Raleigh	24%
5	Will Smith	16%
6	Salvador Perez	9%
7	Shea Langeliers	9%
8	Logan O'Hoppe	7%
9	Francisco Alvarez	7%
10	Willson Contreras	7%
11	Tyler Stephenson	6%
12	J.T. Realmuto	-1%
13	Ryan Jeffers	-5%
14	Sean Murphy	-7%
15	Austin Wells	-7%
16	Conor Wong	-7%
17	Keibert Ruiz	-13%
18	Gabriel Moreno	-16%
19	Jonah Heim	-18%
20	Joey Bart	-19%
21	Travis d'Arnaud	-25%
22	Partick Bailey	-27%
23	Alejandro Kirk	-27%
24	Mitch Garver	-29%

***Get updated RPV Cheat for one time $5 cost (free updates)
PayPal: FantasyBlackBook@gmail.com or Venmo: @FantasyBlackBook
And include your email address***

Player Profiles and Overview

By Brian Entrekin

Catcher used to be the position most fantasy managers pass over. It's a position where most would wait till the end of drafts to fill the catcher roster spots. With the fantasy game evolving and more leagues playing with two catchers, the need to draft an elite option has become a bigger deal. Drafting an elite option can give your fantasy team a jump start on the rest of the league. Now, if you are not in a two-catcher league, you can still wait at the catcher's position, and you should be just fine.

When looking back at the catcher position for the 2024 season, we saw many catchers rack up playing time thanks to the universal DH. Twenty-four catchers played over 100 games, and 38 catchers played over 80 games. Nine catchers had 500+ plate appearances, and 16 had at least 400, which is excellent for counting stats. We also saw many young catchers have an impact later in the season, with plenty more that may debut in 2025.

When looking into the 2025 season, the position is more profound than ever. I am comfortable rostering a solid 12 catchers while still sleeping well at night with others in the Top 20. The youth movement at the position is excellent, allowing for more speculation. Building your rosters has dramatically changed with the depth at catcher, making drafts and roster building even more fun this season.

The Elite

1. **William Contreras, MIL (G: 120 C | 35 DH):** Contreras ended the 2023 season as one of the best fantasy catchers in the game, and he backed that up in 2024 with an even better season. He hit .281 with a career-high in home runs with 23, RBIs with 92, runs with 99, and even steals with nine. Contreras was a great 5-category contributor while improving his walk rate to 11.5%, giving him a .365 OBP, his third straight year with an OBP over .350. The Brewers want him in the lineup as much as possible, which led to a league-wide 679 plate appearances for a catcher. He will be 27 in 2025 and should be in line for another great fantasy season.

2. **Adley Rutschman, BAL (G: 103 C | 45 DH):** In his third season with the Orioles, Rutschman had a good season but was a step back from 2023. In 2024, Rutschman hit .250 with 19 home runs, 68 runs scored, and 79 RBIs. Those were all lower from 2023. Rutshman was also known for an elite walk rate, which dropped to 9.1% from a 13.4% walk rate in 2023. There may be a good reason for Rutschman's struggles, as he suffered a couple of injuries in the second half of the season, which was in line with his production dropping. Rutschman will continue to receive plenty of plate appearances, making Rutschman one of the elite fantasy catchers in the game.

3. **Yanier Diaz, HOU (G: 102 C | 37 DH | 11 1B):** After a strong rookie season in 2023, Diaz got off to a slow start, leaving fantasy managers frustrated. Those who stuck with him were rewarded with a strong second half to the season. Diaz hit .319 with nine home runs and 35 RBI over 63 games in the second half of the season. The solid second half left him with a season stat line of .299/16/70/84/2. A .299 batting average over 148 games from a catcher is outstanding. Diaz will be 26 years old this season, and he should be in line for another great season hitting in the middle of the Astros lineup.

4. **Salvador Perez, KC (G: 91 C | 49 1B | 23 DH):** Salvador Perez keeps getting older, and his fantasy production continues to be great. This past season, Perez hit .271 with 27 home runs and 104 RBI while playing in 158 games, the most by any catcher. It was the eighth straight season (not counting 2020) where Perez hit at least 20 home runs and the fourth consecutive year hitting at least .250 with 75+ RBI. He even improved his plate discipline, walking 6.7% of the time, up from 3.3% last season, lowering his strike-out rate from 23.3% to 19.8%. Perez keeps getting older, but the Royals find plenty of ways to get his bat in the lineup, which keeps him as one of the top fantasy catchers in the game.

Top Talent

1. **Will Smith, LAD (G: C 121 | 3 DH):** Smith started the season strong but hit the skids through June, July, and August, leaving many fantasy managers frustrated. He picked things up over the season's final month and ended the 2024 year with another productive season. Smith hit .248 with 20 home runs, 77 runs and 75 RBI. It was Smith's fourth straight year with at least 19 home runs, 70 runs scored, and 75 RBI. He continues to be a consistent force at the catching position, and his production should continue to be strong while hitting in the Dodgers lineup.

2. **Willson Contreras, STL (G: 51 C | 33 DH):** Contreras suffered through an injury-riddled 2024, where he only played in 84 games after playing at least 100 games every season since 2016. Even with the shortened season, Contreras hit .262 with 15 home runs. His career-high walk rate of 12.6% gave him a career-high .380 OBP. Contreras's significant injury in 2024 was due to a hit-by-pitch, so we should expect a healthy version of him in 2025. The Cardinals want him to play more and plan on using Contreras at 1B, upping Contreras's fantasy appeal.

3. **J.T. Realmuto, PHI (G: 99 C):** Realmuto only played 99 games in 2024 due to a knee injury that placed him on the IL for a while. His production was definitely affected by the injury, as Realmuto only stole two bases after stealing at least 13 bases over the last three seasons. He still hit 14 home runs with a .266 batting average, which was fine and gives optimism for a strong 2025. When healthy, Realmuto will hit in the middle of a loaded Phillies lineup, which should provide plenty of fantasy goodness.

4. **Logan O'Hoppe, LAA (G: 127 C | 7 DH):** In his first season playing over 100 games, O'Hoppe put together a great season. He hit .244 with 20 home runs, 64 runs scored, and 56 RBI. His 12% barrel rate and 46.3% hard-hit rate are great for O'Hoppe, and it was his second season producing strong quality of contact metrics. The power and respectable batting average is legit, but the run production will depend on a suspect team around him. O'Hoppe's skills are good, leaving a nice fantasy floor with plenty of upside. O'Hoppe will be the primary catcher for the Angels again, and we could see better things in his age-25 season.

5. **Cal Raleigh, SEA (G: 135 C | 19 DH):** In 2024, Raleigh proved to be a powerful fantasy catcher once again. Raleigh hit 34 home runs with 73 runs scored and 100 RBI. It was his third straight year with at least 27 home runs while providing 70+ runs and RBIs over the last two seasons. The weakness for Raleigh is his batting average, as he hit .220 this past season after hitting .232 in 2023, which was a career-high. Raleigh will continue to provide plenty of power and run production, but you have to be smart while drafting, as his batting average could hurt your team.

6. **Tyler Stephenson, CIN (G: 127 C | 9 DH):** After a mediocre 2023, Stephenson returned with a powerful 2024. He hit 19 home runs with 69 runs and 66 RBI while batting .258. The .258 batting average is very nice for the catching position to go with plenty of power. Stephenson also lowered his strikeout rate to

22.7% from 26.1%, which likely aided in his improved batting average. A 9.1% barrel rate aided the improvement in power, which has been Stephenson's best since 2020. Stephenson can potentially be a breakout fantasy catcher with his overall skill set and playing half of his games in Great American Small Park.

7. **Keibert Ruiz, WAS (G: 116 C | 9 DH):** Ruiz had a down season as he hit .229 with 13 home runs, but there was a good reason for the struggles. Ruiz was ill in the middle of the season, missing a couple of weeks and losing a lot of weight, which he had to put back on while playing. Once healthy, Ruiz hit .277 over the season's final month, showcasing the great hit tool we've come to expect from Ruiz. A healthy Ruiz provides 15 home runs and a strong batting average at the catcher position, making for a nice mid-round catching target.

8. **Shea Langeliers, ATH (G: 131 C | 3 DH):** Shea Bangeliers had a big boy season. After hitting .218 and .205 in his first two seasons, Langeliers hit .224, which is not great but works for a catcher like Langeliers. It works because of his power, which he showcased, hitting 29 home runs and driving in 80 runs. Langeliers had a 12.8% barrel rate and a 44% hard-hit rate, which is great for power, but also an xBA of .244, showing room for more fantasy goodness. At worst, Langeliers is a poor man's Cal Raleigh with plenty of room for improvement.

9. **Austin Wells, NYY (G: 110 C | 2 DH):** Wells finished his rookie season hitting .229 with 13 home runs, 42 runs scored, and 55 RBI. He struggled in the season's final month, but in July and August, he hit .303 with nine home runs, showcasing the skill set that many prospect folks thought Wells possessed. He should continue hitting in the middle of the Yankees' batting order, again bringing plenty of run production.

Solid Options

1. Francisco Alvarez, NYM (G: 96 C | 3 DH): After hitting 25 home runs in 2023, Alvarez took a step back with 11 home runs. He did improve his batting average from .209 to .237, but it was still a letdown season. Some of the difficulties were due to injuries. Alvarez will be 23 in 2025, and a healthy season could result in another 20+ home runs, which is rare at the catcher position. The floor is unstable, but his ceiling is very high if the youngster can figure it out.

2. Joey Bart, PIT (G: 69 C | 11 DH): Bart proved that a change of scenery is sometimes a good thing. Over 80 games, Bart hit 13 home runs with 45 RBI while hitting .265. Injuries were the only thing that limited his season. He brings a solid batting average with a lot of power upside, hitting in the middle of the Pirates lineup. A great C2 draft pick with a C1 upside.

3. Alejandro Kirk, TOR (G: 93 C | 5 DH): For the last few seasons, Kirk was in a platoon with Danny Jansen, but that has come to an end. He finished last season hitting .253 with only five home runs. The batting average skills and plate discipline are what many love from Kirk, and the power should get better. Just two seasons ago, Kirk hit 14 home runs over 139 games. He can potentially return to his 2023 form, making him a strong C2.

4. Jonah Heim, TEX (G: 119 G | 13 DH): After a monster 2023 season, Heim regressed quite a bit. He hit .220 with 13 home runs and 59 RBI, a massive drop from 2023 when he hit .258 with 18 home runs and 95 RBI. Heim's groundball rate rose to 42.4%, and his barrel rate dropped two points, which were significant factors in the drop in production. Heim should still be a viable fantasy catcher, but not the elite fantasy catcher some hoped for after 2023.

5. Gabriel Moreno, ARI (G: 93 C | 1 3B): Moreno is Alejandro Kirk's doppleganger. This past season, he missed time due to injury but still hit five home runs and had a .266 batting average. Moreno improved his walk rate from 7.6% to 11.7% while striking out only 14.8% of the time, down from 19.7%. His barrel rate improved to 6.6%, but a ground ball rate near 50% will limit his overall power potential. Moreno provides a robust skill set at the plate and a strong batting average, but the power may be lacking for a great fantasy catcher.

Red Flags

1. Henry Davis, PIT (G: 34 C | 1 DH): Many were excited for Davis in 2024 and disappointed. In his limited time with the Pirates, Davis hit .144 while striking out 36.9% of the time. Due to his struggles, Davis spent most of the season at AAA. With Bart becoming the starting pitcher in Pittsburgh, there is no longer a clear path to playing time for Davis, killing his fantasy value.

2. Jake Rogers, DET (G: 92 C | 7 DH): Rogers was once again the Tigers' primary catcher, but the plate production leaves no fantasy value. This past season, he hit .197 with ten home runs and a near 30% strikeout rate. Rogers is best as a backup catcher, and that could happen sooner rather than later, with Dillon Dingler looming to take over the catching duties in Detroit.

3. Ben Rortvedt, TB (G: 111 C): Rortvedt hit .228 last season with three measly home runs. The Rays catching situation has been fantasy death in recent years, which has not changed, with Rortvedt being the primary catcher. He struck out 26.8% of the time with a ground ball rate of 46.3% and a 3.5% barrel rate. It's best to ignore the catching situation in Tampa Bay for fantasy.

4. Luis Campusano, SD (G: 86 C | 2 1B): Campusano was supposed to be the future behind the plate in San Diego. This past season, he only hit .227 with eight home runs and was eventually sent back to AAA as Kyle Higashioka produced at the plate and became the regular catcher in San Diego. For now, Campusano may get a second chance at the job, but Ethan Salas is looming to take over the role for years to come.

Up and Coming

1. Adrian Del Castillo, ARI (G: 24 C): Del Castillo got his first cup of coffee with the DBacks this past year and hit .313 with four home runs, filling in for an injured Gabriel Moreno. At AAA, Del Castillo hit .312 with 26 home runs. Del Castillo could be a fantasy stud in 2025 if Moreno struggles or gets hurt again.

2. Dillon Dingler, DET (G: 27 C): Dingler only hit .167 with one home run while striking out 34.5% of the time in limited action with the Tigers in 2024. It was a different story at AAA, as Dingler hit .308 with 17 home runs while striking out 20.3% of the time. Rogers should not hold Dingler back for long, making the latter someone to keep an eye on in 2025.

3. Samuel Basallo, BAL (G: 0): Between AA and AAA this past season, Basallo hit .278 with 19 home runs and ten steals. Adley Rutschman has the Baltimore catching position locked down, but Basallo could see some time late in the season. He is also rumored to be a trade asset, which could make him fantasy viable on another team. The skills are there; just looking for playing time.

4. Dalton Rushing, LAD (G: 0): The Dodgers have Will Smith as the primary catcher in LA, but we've seen backup Austin Barnes play 50-60 games in recent seasons. Rushing hit .271 with 26 home runs between AA and AAA. Rushing is better than Barnes, leaving an opening for Rushing to have an impact in 2025.

5. Edgar Quero, CWS (G: 0): The White Sox are starting the season with Korey Lee at catcher, leaving plenty of potential for an opening. Quero could be that guy who takes the opportunity and runs with it. Between AA and AAA last year, Quero hit 16 home runs while hitting .280. There's a good chance he sees a good amount of playing time this year, especially in the second half.

6. Drake Baldwin, ATL (G: 0): With Travis d'Arnaud not returning to the Braves, there is a need for a backup catcher. Last year, Baldwin hit .276 with 16 home runs between AA and AAA. He could become a backup with the Braves, and in recent years, the backup has seen plenty of playing time.

7. Moises Ballesteros, CHC (G: 0): With Miguel Amaya's inconsistencies in Chicago, not to mention an unclear backup, Ballesteros could see his first taste of the big leagues in 2025. Last year, he hit 19 home runs between AA and AAA while hitting .289. He continued his hot hitting in the Arizona Fall League, where Ballesteros hit .317 with five home runs. He's the future backstop with the Cubs, which could begin this year.

8. Agustin Ramirez, MIA (G: 0): Ramirez was traded to the Marlins from the Yankees last season and had a massive season in the minors. Between AA and AAA, Ramirez hit 25 home runs while hitting .267. The Marlins have Nick Fortes as their primary catcher, which should only hold Ramirez back for a short time.

Serviceable

1. Sean Murphy, ATL (G: 69C): Last season was brutal for Murphy, as he battled injuries and only played in 72 games. Murphy hit .193 with ten home runs and a career-low 36.5% hard-hit rate. A healthy Murphy makes for a nice back-end C1, but more likely a C2. He just needs to stay healthy, which he has not done in the last two seasons.

2. Ivan Herrera, STL (G: 56 C | 12 DH): Herrera had a solid season filling in for an injured Willson Contreras. Over 72 games, he hit .301 with five home runs and five steals. He had a good .127 ISO, a strong .372 OBP, and a great 127 wRC+. Herrera should see plenty of playing time in 2025, with Contreras moving to more playing time at 1B.

3. Bo Naylor, CLE (G: 115 C | 4 DH): After a nice debut run in 2023, Naylor took a step back in 2024. He hit .201 with 13 home runs and six stolen bases. His plate discipline struggled as he struck out 31.4% of the time with a significant drop in contact rates and a 12.4% SwStr. Naylor will be 25, so there is plenty of room to grow, and he could be in for a bounce-back season as he will once again be the primary catcher in Cleveland.

4. Ryan Jeffers, MIN (G: 86 C | 34 DH): Jeffers was on fire to start the season but finished hitting .226 with 21 home runs and splitting time with Christian Vazquez. Jeffers will again be Minnesota's primary catcher, and an entire season of consistent production could lead to a great fantasy season from Jeffers.

5. Patrick Bailey, SF (G: 115 C | 3 DH): Bailey battled injuries in 2024, which once again limited his production. He finished hitting .234 with eight home runs. Bailey's defense is elite, which will keep him in the lineup for 125+ games, making him a viable C2 when he's swinging it well.

6. Hunter Goodman, COL (23 C | 34 OF | 11 DH | 4 1B): After a struggle to find playing time in the outfield for the Rockies, Goodman found his way to a regular catching role once Elias Diaz was DFA'd. Goodman finished with 13 home runs, but a 3.6% walk rate and .190 batting average need improvements. In September, he became the Rockies' primary catcher, hitting .226 with five home runs over 17 games. Goodman is one of my favorite late-round gambles at catcher.

7. Miguel Amaya, CHC (116 C): Amaya had high expectations in his first season as the primary catcher with the Cubs. Over 117 games, Amaya hit .232 with eight home runs. He'll start 2025 as the primary catcher, making him a viable C2 option, but Ballesteros is looming if Amaya struggles.

8. Connor Wong, BOS (106 C | 14 1B | 9 DH | 6 2B | 1 OF): For a second straight season, Wong proved to be a strong C2 in all formats. He hit .280 with 13 home runs and eight stolen bases while also combining for 106 runs and RBI. Wong plays all over the diamond, which keeps his bat in the lineup and provides plenty of fantasy upside.

9. Kyle Higashioka, FA (83 C): Higashioka started the season backing up Campusano but ultimately took over the primary catching role for the Padres. He finished the year hitting .220 with 17 home runs. Higashioka is a free agent, and depending on what team he signs with, he could provide some late-round fantasy appeal.

10. Freddy Fermin, KC (91 C | 21 DH): Fermin is technically the backup catcher to Salvador Perez, but that does not mean he is not fantasy-relevant. He played in 111 games in 2024 after playing in 70 games in 2023. Last year, Fermin hit .271 with six home runs after hitting .281 with nine home runs in 2023. He provides a great batting average source in the later rounds.

AL/NL Only

1. Victor Caratini, HOU (G: 58 C | 11 1B | 3 DH): Caratini has played at least 87 games in three of the last four years. This past year, he hit .269 with eight home runs in his first season with the Astros. With Yanier Diaz playing DH occasionally and Caratini playing some first base, he becomes fantasy-relevant in AL-only leagues.

2. Jose Trevino, NYY (G: 71 C): Austin Wells will be the primary catcher for the Yankees, but Trevino should face most LHP, giving him the chance to play 60-70 games. This past season, Trevino hit .215 with eight home runs. He's not a world-beater, but hitting in the Yankees lineup keeps him AL-only relevant in his limited role.

3. Danny Jansen, BOS (G: 82 C | 6 DH): For an only-league catcher, Jansen brings excellent power, hitting double-digit home runs from 2021-23 and nine this past season. He'll be a back up in Boston.

4. Travis d'Arnaud, LAA (G: 89 C): d'Arnaud has been one of the better backups in baseball in recent years. He hit .238 this past year with 15 home runs over 99 games. d'Arnaud has played in 74 or more games in the last three years with at least 11 home runs. He'll be a backup again, primarily playing versus LHP with the Angels, which could bring AL-only appeal.

5. Korey Lee, CWS (G: 113 C | 9 DH): In his first year as the primary catcher for the White Sox, Lee played in 125 games, hitting .210 with 12 home runs. He'll again start the season as the lead backstop, making him a strong AL-only target.

6. Pedro Pages, STL (G: 66 C | 1 1B): Herrera should be the primary benefactor to Contreras playing more first base, but Pages may get some fantasy love too. This past season, Pages played in 66 games, hitting .238 with seven home runs and two steals. If anything happens to Herrera or the Cardinals change things up behind the plate, Pages could get a more significant fantasy role.

7. Gary Sanchez, FA (G: 28 C | 48 DH | 4 1B): Sanchez once again provided solid only-league fantasy value in 2024, where he hit .220 with 11 home runs. Sanchez has double-digit home runs each year since 2016 and has played at least 75 games each season since 2017, not counting 2020. He's a free agent but will find a home somewhere, and he could once again be an only-league late-round target.

8. Elias Diaz, FA (G: 79 C | 16 DH): Diaz has been a serviceable fantasy catcher in recent years, but he lost his starting role, was DFA'd and then traded to be a backup catcher last year. Diaz still hit .265 with six home runs, but as a free agent, it may be tough to get a full-time role, making Diaz an only-league target these days.

9. Christian Vázquez, MIN (G: 86 C | 3 3B | 3 DH | 1 1B): Vazquez has played at least 93 games yearly since 2019. This past season, he hit .221 with seven home runs and three steals. He should be backing up Jeffers again this season, making Vazquez an AL-only league target again.

10. Nick Fortes, MIA (G: 109 C): Fortes has played at least 108 games in the last two seasons. This past year, he hit .227 with four home runs. The offensive production is limited, but the at-bats are there in Miami, and those at-bats are king in only leagues.

Chapter 6

First Basemen

	Leagues w/o CINF	RPV
1	Vladimir Guerrero	29%
2	Bryce Harper	18%
3	Freddie Freeman	16%
4	Matt Olson	6%
5	Pete Alonso	5%
6	Josh Naylor	3%
7	Christian Walker	2%
8	Spencer Steer	-2%
9	Cody Bellinger	-3%
10	Triston Casas	-4%
11	Paul Goldschmidt	-8%
12	Vinny Pasquantino	-10%
13	Issac Paredes	-11%
14	Jake Burger	-13%
15	Yandy Diaz	-13%
16	Alec Bohm	-15%

	Leagues w/ CINF	RPV
1	Vladimir Guerrero	37%
2	Bryce Harper	26%
3	Freddie Freeman	24%
4	Matt Olson	13%
5	Pete Alonso	12%
6	Josh Naylor	10%
7	Christian Walker	10%
8	Spencer Steer	5%
9	Cody Bellinger	4%
10	Triston Casas	3%
11	Paul Goldschmidt	-2%
12	Vinny Pasquantino	-3%
13	Issac Paredes	-4%
14	Jake Burger	-7%
15	Yandy Diaz	-7%
16	Alec Bohm	-9%
17	Ryan Mountcastle	-7%
18	Rhys Hoskins	-9%
19	Nolan Schanuel	-14%
20	Josh Bell	-14%
21	Nate Lowe	-15%
22	Michael Busch	-15%
23	Kyle Manzardo	-18%
24	Jake Cronenworth	-18%

***Get updated RPV Cheat for one time $5 cost (free updates)
PayPal: FantasyBlackBook@gmail.com or Venmo: @FantasyBlackBook
And include your email address***

First Baseman Profiles and Overview
By Chris Welsh

2024 did not bring the firepower that we are used to from first base. We didn't have a 50-home-run hitter, a 40-home-run hitter, or even a first baseman that clocked in at 35 home runs. We did see some batting avengers come up on a few players, which makes the gap between the low-average big home run guys and the more well-balanced a bit wider. We also lost quite a few of the first-base guys who were stealing bags. Those stolen bases could add up when getting them at a position you normally don't get at. Spencer Steer was the only qualified first baseman to hit 20 home runs and steal 20 bases, while only one other player hit 20 and stole 10, that being Paul Goldschmidt. NFBC early drafts have nine qualified players at first base going inside the top-100, and just 17 total inside the top 200. That shows you the value of some of the big bats are coming down. That also puts more emphasis on high-power, high-average bats. Power has become the new stolen base arms race, so prioritizing the quality big bats early seems like a smart strategy.

The Elite

1. **Vladimir Guerrero Jr., TOR (G: 121 1B | 12 3B):** Vladdy Jr has struggled to string great years together, but 2024 looks to be the best year yet for him to continue his success. Vlad Jr led all first basemen with a 5.5 WAR, had a career-high batting average at .323, and was the only first baseman to hit 30 home runs with 90 or more RBI and runs. He was in the 97th percentile of the league in xwOBA, xBA, xSLG, hard hit percentage, and average exit velocity. Though his launch angle dropped, the quality of contact went up, posting a 13.7% barrel percentage, the second-best of his career and in the 90th percentile of the league. The quality of contact is essential for Vlad. He improved his average against all pitch types. He also decided to stop forcing pulled balls. The previous year, he had a 38% pull rate, which dropped to 33% this year, which was the lowest of his career. This shows up in his spray chart as he puts the ball to the opposite field more than ever. Vlad seems more comfortable as a hitter than ever before. That is saying something for a guy who also struck out only 13% of the time, which was another career low. Early projections are already favorable for him to push close to a 35/100/100 season. Vladdy Jr has established himself as the top first baseman in 2025 and somewhere in the middle of the second round in drafts.

2. **Bryce Harper, PHI (G: 141 1B):** The game has always been about keeping Harper healthy because when he's out there, he's a first to second-round fantasy pick. Now that he's playing first base exclusively, we can dream of 140-plus games yearly. This past year was only the second time he's played more than 140 games in the last five years. Besides a July to forget, Harper hit .298 or better in four of the season's six months. He was one of only two first baseman to hit 30 home runs with a .280 or better average. Harper also saw an increase in his hard-hit percentage to 48.2%, the highest over the last three years. His ability to attack went up as well, as he increased his zone contact percentage by more than six percentage points. Where he struggled seemed to be hitting four-seam fastballs, seeing a 30 batting average points dip. Pitchers also increased their sinker usage against him, as he saw it three percent more this year, which was the biggest increase of any pitch and led to the rise in GIDP. His barrel percentage dipped to the second lowest of his career, but it was still over 10% and is likely related to his ability to hit four seams. The tremendous talent overshadows the minor negative highlights.

3. **Freddie Freeman, LAD (G: 147 1B):** Freeman has been the king of consistency. Three straight years of 100+ runs and hitting over .300, two straight of 100+ RBI, and even a 20/20 season in 2023. In 2024, we saw a production dip across the board. He failed to go over 90 RBI or runs, hit just 22 home runs, and had the lowest batting average of .282 since 2015. Freeman's declines come from the quality of contact, as his barrel percentage fell to 9.1%, the lowest of his career, and his hard hit percentage fell to 41.8%, resulting from a three-year decline and the lowest since 2018. Freeman held his exit velocity against fastballs, as were the launch angle and whiff rate. In 2023, he hit .344 against fastballs, according to BaseballSavant, which fell to .287 in 2024. As unsatisfying as it is, much of his tiny dips in production read as an age decline. A more satisfying answer may also be his decline against lefties, where he hit over .300 in 2023 but just .250 this past year. Freeman also destroyed inside pitches the previous year, with averages of over .400 and .500 on a zone chart. The previous year, he had an over 80% swing rate on inside pitches in the upper zone, which dropped to under 80 and 60% in the different quadrants. Struggles on inside pitches, which led to less barreling, declining hard-hit numbers, and struggles against lefties are just some pieces that ultimately speak to a mid-30s player starting a decline. Much of Freeman's game is intact, so he is no fade when hitting behind Mookie Betts and Shohei Ohtani. He may just be a better second or third-round player with a high batting average upside.

Top Talent

1. **Matt Olson, ATL (G: 162 1B):** Olson's 2023 was one for the ages as he hit over .280 with 53 home runs. What seems more likely now is that the season was the outlier rather than the new standard. We saw cuts across the board for Olson. He hit a little over half of what he did the year prior with 29, dropped his average by almost 40 points, and saw a massive decrease in his hard-hit percentage from 55% to 47%. Pitchers didn't pitch to him in a dramatically different way, but he vastly underperformed against four-seam fastballs, going from .312 down to .252 this past year. This again points to the 2023 season being the vastly over-performed season. One thing to watch with Olson during the season is how he hits righties. This year, he hit lefties better than righties, .263 vs .240. In his big 2023, he hit .293 against righties. He also seems to have a little "every other year" thing going with how he hits righties. This could mean he makes that a bigger focus when he struggles, and when he hits well, it's on to other things. That's just a guess. There is an upside as his cost should come down. Projections early on see him similar to last year as a 35/100/100 type player with a .250 average.

2. **Pete Alonso, FA (G: 161 1B):** After a year where the top first baseman in 2023 hit more than 50 home runs, it's wild to say that Alonso led first base with 34 home runs in 2024. That was 12 home runs fewer than the prior year, and he could only manage a .217 average. This year's average represented his xBA from the preceding year (.240) and his 2024 xBA of .242. Alonso's hard-hit percentage was 46.4, the second-highest of his career. It works well with his 75.3 mph bat speed, which ranks in the 93rd percentile of the league. Though his average went up, one thing the league caught up to year-over-year was to pitch him more sliders. Alonso saw the biggest increase in sliders, which he hit worse this year than the previous year at just .160. All the bat speed in the world won't help him in that department. Alonso is very much what we think. He is a .240 hitter who can put up 40 home runs in his sleep. His lack of average and the volatility that comes with it likely keep him out of the first three rounds.

Solid Options

1. **Triston Casas, BOS (G: 61 1B):** Casas finished the year with a .241 average and 13 home runs in 212 at-bats. You don't want to make excuses for players, but this is one that you can almost just throw away due to injury. Casas suffered torn cartilage in the rib area. He returned for a little part of the back half of the year but also had shoulder inflammation. His hard-hit numbers stayed true, as did his ability to barrel. He lost five degrees on his launch angle, which I think speaks to the injury more than anything. Casas is on the higher end of bat speed in the league, so he was probably dealing with a level of compensation towards that as well. He struggled some with off-speed in the last month of the season, where his average dipped. However, Steamer projections are optimistic he's still the great up-and-coming young star and the injury will be behind him, projecting almost 30 home runs and a .245 batting average. His early draft ADP puts him around 100 overall, which could make him a big first baseman power target past round five or six.

2. **Josh Naylor, ARI (G: 137 1B):** Naylor was one of four first basemen to hit 30 or more home runs but led all at the position with 108 RBI. Naylor's power didn't shine in 2023, but he had some expected stats that screamed offensive growth. That happened in the form of a career-high in home runs, but it came at the expense of his average. His average dipped close to 60 points as he sold out for more power. Most of his underlying numbers held in the form of barreling and hard hit. This helps power his xBA, which was around 10 points higher than his actual average and creates more optimism that he cannot only be an annual 30-home-run hitter but also recoup that above-position batting average.

3. **Christian Walker, FA (G: 129 1B):** Walker, from an AVG/OBP/SLG standpoint, repeated mostly what we know. He suffered a dip in power, dropping down to 26 home runs and a three-year low on RBI at 84 and runs at just 72. Walker's underlying stats held up incredibly well as he finished in the 80th to 90th percentile in xWoba, xSLG, and AVG Exit Velocity. He increased his barrel percentage from 11.4 to 13.1% and his hard hit percentage from 40.4 to 48% hard hit. Two things that stand out are his horrid second half, where he hit .264 in the first and just .207 in the second half. The second was the impact he had against four-seam fastballs. In 2023, he hit .280 with an eight-run value against fastballs. In 2024, he just .230 with a zero value. The positive news is his xBA against was higher, and he had a better xWOBA versus four-seam fastballs than the prior year. Despite the dip in the big counting stats, Walker has underlying stats that give optimism to him becoming a 30-home-run hitter again as long as he signs with a team with at least a league-average home-hitting park.

4. **Luis Arraez, SD (G: 69 1B | 42 2B):** Arraez continues to be a polarizing fantasy player. On the one hand, he's a phenomenal points-league player. He finished his second 200-hit season, his fourth .300 batting average season over the last five years, and a career-low 4.3% strikeout percentage. On the other hand, he comes out as a one or, at best, a two of the five-category player. His average is elite, and his 83 runs are very solid. Unfortunately, he just completed his third straight season of having 12 or 13 combined home runs and stolen bases. He's also close to nothing in the RBI department. He has two consecutive years of putting up under 50 RBI, and over the last three years, he has had a combined 161 RBIs. That is 17 more RBI than what Aaron Judge put up in 2024. In a standard category league, he is a huge deficit in the power department but can single-handedly carry your batting average if you have a lot of power. Arraez is a great target and a starting first baseman in points leagues.

5. **Vinnie Pasquantino, KCR (G: 103 1B):** Pasquantino finally put up his first season of over 100 games played. Besides his average, he put up career highs in home runs at 19, runs at 64, and RBI at 97. His .262 batting average was supported by a .266 xBA and one of the league's lowest strikeout rates at 12.8%. Pasquantino improved his hard hit rate year over year from 40..3% to 46.5%. Staying with the hard hit rate, Pasquantino had a higher hard hit percentage against all pitch types he sees 10% or more of the time. Though Pasquantino played a little less than half of the at-bats in the second half versus the first, he finished with a batting average of 50 points higher and an almost 100-point rise in his OPS. Pasquantino's stabilized average, improved hard-hit numbers, and low strikeout rate gives him a great floor and a position with many ups and downs. If he can become a 30-home-run hitter, he will be a massive value at his early draft costs.

6. **Jake Burger, MIA (G: 69 1B | 59 3B):** Burger is the modern-day Khris Davis, with his third straight year hitting exactly .250. He's also a significant power threat, hitting 34 and 29 home runs in consecutive years. His overall plate of Baseball Savant numbers we look at is thriving. He was essentially in the 80th percentile in xSLG, AVG EV, Hard Hit, and barreling while posting above-average xBA and xwOBA percentages. Burger saw a slight drop-off in a few key areas that could raise an eyebrow. His barrel percentage dropped from 16.7% to 12.3%, and his hard hit rate dropped from 49.6 to 46.8%; his counting stats mostly stayed the same. Where he did improve was cutting his strikeout percentage from 27.6% to 25.9%. He has now seen a strikeout decline in four straight seasons. Despite the earlier declines, Burger is a yearly improving player for the better, dropping in a few areas in favor of being a more consistent hitter. Early projections have him as almost a Casas clone, but 30 rounds later.

Red Flags

1. **Paul Goldschmidt, NYY (G:150 1B):** Goldy finished 2024 with a .245 average, 22 home runs, 70 runs and just 65 RBI. Besides his rookie year, these were all-time lows. Goldschmidt did have a higher xBA than his average at .255 while posting above-average percentages in the expected stat department. The most encouraging of which was his hard-hit percentage, which was maintained at a high level of 49.6%. Despite the hard-hit numbers, this may be a case of age finally taking its toll. Goldy spent the 2023 off-season looking at recouping bat speed but finished a little above average at 72.5, where the league average is 71.5. He has one of the longer swings at 7.8 feet, where the league average is 7.2 feet. This matters because his strikeout percentage jumped to 26.8%, the highest of his career, and his walk percentage fell to 7.6%, which is also the worst of his career. Goldschmidt hit quite a bit better on the road, posting a .260+ average versus a .220 average at home. Overall, he looks to be an average to near below-average bet at first base regardless, but in the Bronx favorable park, he could be an interesting pick post-200.

2. **Christian Encarnacion-Strand, CIN (G: 29 1B):** Strand suffered a wrist injury in April that stopped the season after a few games in May. You have to throw out 2024 with CES. In 2023, he had a fantastic 10% barrel% and a 48% hard-hit rate, with an expected batting average of a little over .240. He was pacing out to be a 25+ home run hitter in one of the friendliest ballparks. We have to throw out last year because everything across the board was a dramatic fall due to that injury. He got into the Arizona Fall League at the end of the season. He hit .385 in eight games but had only two extra-base hits and still sported a 28% strikeout rate. One concern from the 2024 season was a massive increase in his groundball rate, which was carried into the fall league. This, again, can be a repercussion of the wrist injury, but it puts an overall red flag over CES for the coming year. He also has been put out into the outfield, which is not a natural spot. If he struggles, he could lose some playing time or become some form of a platoon. His post-200 ADP will help soften the blow if you decide to invest so he can return to his 2023 production.

Serviceable

1. **Michael Busch, CHC (G: 142 1B | 3 3B | 1 2B):** Busch put up the 10th-best WAR season of any first baseman in 2024. He had a .248 average and 21 home runs in 152 games. Busch doesn't have much to pull from in 2023, but in his first full year, he raised his barrel percentage from 6.5 to 11.2%, his launch angle from 4 degrees to over 17, and lowered his strikeout percentage from 33% to 28%. Busch put up pretty weak hard-hit numbers at just 39% and had an xBA of just .217. He had just a 68 zone swing rate, which, along with a high walk rate and strikeout rate, shows he lacks aggression at the plate. Busch seems likely to have a floor of 20 home runs, 70/70, and around a .240 batting average. He makes for a solid corner infield target.

2. **Michael Toglia, COL (G: 107 1B | 16 OF):** Toglia (pronounced like the G isn't there) hit 25 home runs and stole 10 bases in just 116 games while hitting only .218. He's striking out 32% of the time, which is an issue, and he is essentially a fastball hitter. He hit under .200 against any non-fastball. The reason to get excited is the very red Baseball Savant page. He ranked in the 90th percentile of the league in xWOBA, xSLG, Hard Hit, barrel percentage, and walk percentage. His 17% barrel percentage, paired with a 50.2% hard-hit rate, is what the big power hitters are made of. His expected average was over 20 points higher, with an xBA of .244. Hitting in Colorado with that kind of power and a .240 average could lead to a massive breakout. He also didn't show off the "I only hit in Colorado" split we see with players. Seventeen of his home runs came on the road. Toglia's Steamer projections have him at 27 home runs and a .224 average. If he improves his contact rate, hits a little more non-fastballs, and strikes out a bit less in Colorado, he could hit 40 home runs. He's a great home run chase outside the top 200 of drafts.

3. **Nathaniel Lowe, WAS (G: 138 1B):** Lowe is the definition of the "serviceable" first baseman. Nothing special and nothing really awful. He hit .265 with 16 home runs in 140 games. He hit .260 in the first and second half of the year while hitting .275 or higher in four regular season months. He's a below-average barrel and hard-hit hitter, which isn't ideal for a first baseman. He sports a lower-ish 62% zone swing percentage, which, if he could become more aggressive, you could envision a more impactful hitter with his solid average numbers. He's a boost in OBP as he had a 12% walk rate. Steamer projections see him as the most league-average guy with a .260 average, 20 home runs, and going 75/75 in the run and RBI department. Lowe now finds himself on a young, up and coming Nats team and could see an uptick in RBI and run opportunities, but he has the feel of a corner infielder than a starting fantasy first baseman.

4. **Yandy Diaz, TB (G: 112 1B):** If you just looked at Yandy's average with his Baseball Savant page, you'd think he was one of the better first basemen in the league. The problem is that the counting stats read closer to Luis Arraez. Diaz hit just 14 home runs in 145 games to go with 55 runs and 65 RBI. Diaz hits the ball hard with a 48.7% hard-hit rate and a 117.4 max EV, which is elite. The problem is he doesn't barrel up the ball; it's at just 7.6%, about two percent less than the previous year. He also doesn't get the ball in the air, sporting just a 5-degree launch angle, which is well below average. While he hit the ball hard, his impact generally went down year over year. You can see that in his average against the top pitch types he saw. He had a dip across the board of around 20-30 batting average points and a 55% ground ball rate. He has never had a ground ball rate under 50%. That takes the top off of a big counting stat breakout season. We might see different results if he started pulling the ball in the air. Since that isn't happening, he is a better option in points leagues than Roto.

AL/NL Only

1. **Ryan Mountcastle, BAL (G: 114 1B):** Mountcastle finished 2024 with a .271 average. This is the second straight season with at least a .270 average and the third consecutive year with an xBA of .270 or higher. He did a great job swinging more in the zone while raising his zone contact percentage and maintaining his normal strikeout rate. He hit only 13 home runs this year as his barrel percentage and launch angle dipped. According to Baseball Savant, he had an expected home run total of +4 (four more home runs). The Orioles are also changing the left-field dimensions, which should benefit right-handed hitters. Early Steamer projections already have him at 21 home runs, but if he continues to hit for a high average and builds back up that barrel percentage, it's possible he could crack 25 and become one of the better late-round values at first base.

2. **Rhys Hoskins, MLW (G: 94 1B):** Hoskins finished with 26 home runs and 82 RBI after missing the 2023 season. This would look good if he didn't pair it with a .218 average and the lowest amount of runs scored in a season where he played at least 107 games or more at just 59. Hoskins' xBA was worse than his average at just .202. His strikeout percentage went up to 28%, and his hard-hit rate fell to 42.2%, the lowest since 2019. He barreled the ball better than the previous two years and had a career-high pull rate of 52% to go with a 20-degree launch angle. He ran a more than 20-point lower BABIP, which could help tell a story of how he'll be better in 2025. You also could argue losing the year before set him back. His long, slower swing with worsening strikeout and hard-hit numbers put more doubt than optimism. His ADP is friendly at post-300 and still a nice power source.

3. **Andrew Vaughn, CHW (G: 122 1B):** Vaughn finished 2024 with a .246 average and 19 home runs. Despite being on White Sox, which feels like a four-letter word, he showed some signs of growth as a hitter. His xBA supported his average; he raised his barrel percentage a full percentage point and got the ball in the air to a career-high 16.6% launch angle. Most importantly, he got back to hitting righties well, hitting over .280. The rest of his profile is mediocre, and he is a low-on-base guy. We could see a counting stat increase if he had a supporting cast around him. His power numbers might be less than others in the 300+ range, but he's probably safe to be a .250, 20+ HR corner infielder / AL-only first baseman.

4. **Jake Cronenworth, SD (G: 85 1B | 70 2B):** Cronenworth arguably put up his best season in the last three seasons. He had 17 home runs, 83 RBI, 72 runs, and a .241 average. According to FanGraphs, his xBA was over 20 points higher at .263. It was his best xBA since 2021. He struggled on fastballs but had a 40-point plus xBA versus his actual while improving on offspeed stuff. He's returning to being a higher batting average guy with lower strikeouts, which works well for points leagues. His power still struggles, and while he hit better against righties this past year, 16 of his 17 home runs came from righties. He's probably capped out as a max 20 home run hitter with a .260 plus average. If he gets to hit third again this year, he'll be a great source of RBI. He's hard to roster in standard 5x5 leagues outside of points formats.

5. **Spencer Torkelson, DET (G: 90 1B):** It was a rough year for Tork. He put up just 10 home runs, with a .219 average, on top of spending a good portion of the season back in the minors. His barrel percentage dramatically fell from 14.1% to 6.7%, his hard-hit percentage from 50.9% to 39.7%, and an xBA of just .209. Torkelson chased less this year and had a better launch angle, but these are things compensating for a horrible eye at the plate. The question is, was 2023 the outlier with 31 home runs, or was it 2024? I wouldn't be surprised for him to turn around since he is so young, but nothing in his data shows optimism at the moment.

6. **Nolan Schanuel, LAA (G: 144 1B):** Schanuel hit .250 with 13 home runs and 10 stolen bases, primarily out of the leadoff spot in 2024. He's at the league bottom regarding the positive underlying stats we look for in a hitter to break out. His 3.5% barrel percentage ranked ninth-lowest among all qualified hitters, and his 25.3% hard hit percentage ranked fourth-lowest. Due to his hitting out of the leadoff spot and his ability to get on base, he could be a higher-category player if the runs went up. He's mainly a points league player with a 17% strikeout rate and an over 10% walk rate. He does get the ball in the air, so if we see early signs of a barrel and hard-hit rise, maybe a breakout could happen. Otherwise, in category leagues, leave him to AL-only.

Chapter 7

Second Basemen

	Leagues w/o MINF	RPV
1	Mookie Betts	32%
2	Ketel Marte	30%
3	Ozzie Albies	23%
4	Marcus Semien	5%
5	Jose Altuve	5%
6	Matt McLain	1%
7	Luis Garcia	0%
8	Jackson Holliday	-6%
9	Brice Turang	-8%
10	Jordan Westburg	-9%
11	Xander Bogaerts	-10%
12	Nico Hoerner	-12%
13	Jonathan India	-12%
14	Jake Cronenworth	-13%
15	Luis Arraez	-14%
16	Gleyber Torres	-14%

	Leagues w/ MINF	RPV
1	Mookie Betts	43%
2	Ketel Marte	40%
3	Ozzie Albies	33%
4	Marcus Semien	13%
5	Jose Altuve	13%
6	Matt McLain	9%
7	Luis Garcia	8%
8	Jackson Holliday	2%
9	Brice Turang	0%
10	Jordan Westburg	-1%
11	Xander Bogaerts	-3%
12	Nico Hoerner	-5%
13	Jonathan India	-5%
14	Jake Cronenworth	-6%
15	Luis Arraez	-7%
16	Gleyber Torres	-7%
17	Bryson Stott	-8%
18	Isaac Paredes	-9%
19	Colt Keith	-14%
20	Kristian Campbell	-15%
21	Brendan Donovan	-16%
22	Maikel Garcia	-18%
23	Andres Gimenez	-22%
24	Ha-Seong Kim	-23%

***Get updated RPV Cheat for one time $5 cost (free updates)
PayPal: FantasyBlackBook@gmail.com or Venmo: @FantasyBlackBook
And include your email address***

Second Base Profiles & Overview
by Joe Orrico

As you will see, the second base position is a barren wasteland heading into 2025. The most populated tier highlights AL and NL-only options, which should give you a good idea of the depth we are dealing with.

As is the case in most years, getting second base taken care of early will benefit your team. There are some great options in the first few rounds, such as Jose Altuve, Ketel Marte, Ozzie Albies, and Marcus Semien. After that, it becomes a roulette table. You could take your chances on a young player breaking out, such as Jackson Holliday or Colt Keith. Or perhaps an old veteran hitting their stride again, like Jorge Polanco or Thairo Estrada.

One thing is for sure, though. The longer you wait, the less certainty (and guaranteed playing time) there is amongst the following options, making second base the weakest position in fantasy baseball again in 2025.

The Elite

1. **Jose Altuve, HOU (G: 147 2B):** 2024 was another typical Jose Altuve season, again providing elite production across the board and finishing as the No. 2 second baseman in baseball overall. He played 153 games (his most since 2017) and contributed 20 HR, 94 R, 65 RBI, 22 SB, and a robust .295 batting average. He is now 34 years old, and there will be some people who are worried about his decline, but there haven't been many apparent signs that he is on a downward trajectory. While his SwStr% went up to 10.4%, he still struck out just 17.4% of the time. His walk rate was still down in double digits. While his slugging percentage and isolated power (ISO) did drop a bit, he's never relied on raw power alone to get the ball out of the yard. Since Statcast was introduced in 2015, he has had a measly 6.1 barrel% and 31.9% hard-hit rate and has never struggled to hit for power despite it. The Astros' lineup is still very good around him, and early projections from Steamer call for 22 HR and 19 SB. He should continue to be an elite, five-category stud that isn't priced like one. He is going as the No. 3 second baseman off the board in early drafts with an ADP of 57, and he looks like one of the best values at any position.

2. **Ketel Marte, ARI (G: 113 2B, 22 DH, 1 2B):** Marte had a brilliant 2024 campaign. He was one of the better value picks of the season, finishing as the #1 second baseman and the #14 player overall, according to the FanGraphs player rater. This season greatly resembled the 2019 breakout that landed him a 4th place MVP finish in the National League. Marte had 36 HR, 93 R, 95 RBI, and 7 SB, all while batting .292 with a .932 OPS. He made incredible gains in his power metrics, raising his barrel rate from 8.0% to 12.3% and his hard hit rate from 42.8% to 53.3%. While those numbers are fantastic, it's worth noting that Marte has now played 10 major league seasons, and he has been an MVP-level player in two of them. That's not to say that he was bad in the other seasons; he has been a very serviceable fantasy player throughout his career, but it's hard not to see 2024 as a bit of an outlier. Now 31 years old, expecting him to repeat this performance feels like a huge gamble. While he isn't a red flag necessarily, buying into players coming off of a career year is generally bad practice, especially when they come with such an increased price (ADP 28).

3. **Ozzie Albies, ATL (G: 99 2B):** It was a tough season for Albies in a few different ways. He played in 99 games as he dealt with wrist and toe injuries, and his performance was very pedestrian when he could take the field. He had 435 PA and contributed just 10 HR, 52 R, 53 RBI, 8 SB, and a .251 batting average, making him one of the biggest busts of the 2024 season. However, many of his troubles were injury-related, and many numbers below the surface were similar to prior seasons. While his barrel rate and hard-hit percentages dropped a few points, his Max EV of 113.7 was a career-high, and his 18.4-degree launch angle is pretty close to optimal. Even with the injuries, his K% and SwStr% remained intact, and he was 8/9 on SB attempts, even with the nagging toe problem. Still just 27 years of age, there is an excellent opportunity to buy the dip on Albies. As Atlanta prepares to get some significant reinforcements back in the lineup in 2025, a healthy Albies should be able to thrive and threaten for the #1 overall 2B on the year as a rock-solid contributor in all five categories.

Top Talent

1. **Marcus Semien, TEX (G: 159 2B):** Semien is a workhorse, and 2024 was no different. For the seventh consecutive season (excluding the shortened 2020 campaign), Semien eclipsed the 700 PA threshold. He played in 159 games, a number he hasn't gone under in an entire season going back to 2018. However, this was the first year where he started to show his age a bit. The now 34-year-old Semien put up 23 HR, 101 R, 74 RBI, 8 SB, and a .237 batting average. He wasn't bad, still finishing as the #6 2B on the year, but this was a step back after many years of top-tier production. There isn't anything to be overly concerned about in his profile, though. His barrel% (6.6%) and hard-hit rate (35.2%) were essentially the same as they were in 2023, his K% (14.6) remained unchanged, and there was just a small increase to his very good SwStr% (7.8% to 9.5%). There's an argument to be made that it was only a down year for Semien because of a career-worst .250 BABIP, which can be attributed to an increase in his ground ball rate combined with reduced speed as he ages. I think it's very reasonable to expect him to meet, if not exceed, his projections from Steamer (25 HR, 12 SB, .253 batting average). He's coming at a steep discount this season with his current ADP of 90, and he makes for a great target at one of the weaker positions heading into 2025.

Solid Options

1. **Luis Garcia, WSH (G: 129 2B, 8 DH)** Garcia took a step forward in 2024, becoming one of the more dependable options at a barren second base position. Playing in 140 games, Garcia hit 18 HR with 58 R, 70 RBI, 22 SB, and an excellent .282 batting average. He made significant gains in his barrel rate (5.8% to 8.0%) and hard-hit rate (35.7% to 41.2%) while raising his launch angle and improving his max and average exit velocity. Absolutely what you want to see across the board in terms of projecting his power going forward, and early Steamer projections have him hitting another 18 next season. While his sprint speed is pretty mediocre, the Nationals have shown that they aren't afraid to get things moving on the basepaths, and Garcia could make a push for another 20+ SB campaign. There isn't much to say against him. His xBA was within two points of his actual average, he doesn't strike out much, and the Nationals' lineup around him is improving steadily each season. He's a solid option if you miss out on the top tier of talent.

2. **Brice Turang, MIL (G: 152 2B, 1 DH):** After a fairly pedestrian rookie season in 2023, Turang took a big step forward this past season and finished as the 2B4 overall. Playing in 155 games, he finished with 7 HR, 72 R, 57 RBI, 50 SB, and a .254 batting average. Things did tail off down the stretch for him, as Turang hit just .220 with one home run in the second half of the season. However, it was still a very promising campaign that he should be able to use as a building block going forward. Turang's xBA, xSLG, and xwOBA all took a step up from last season, and he was also able to cut his SwStr% from 8.2% to 5.6% while maintaining his solid 8.1 BB%. He should function as the Brewers' leadoff man (at least against RHP), and everything he has achieved is well within reach again. Steamer projections expect him to hit a few more HR while sacrificing a bit of his speed (10 HR/38 SB), and I think most drafters will happily sign up for that around pick 150.

3. **Nico Hoerner, CHC (G: 144 2B, 10 SS):** Hoerner's season may have seemed disappointing on the surface, but his overall production was very similar between 2023 and 2024. Playing in 151 games, he produced 7 HR, 86 R, 48 RBI, 31 SB, and a .273 batting average. Compared to 2023, he was down 2 HR, 12 R, 20 RBI, 12 SB, and 10 points of batting average. It was definitely a worse overall season, but not dramatically different considering public perception. A complicated factor when evaluating Hoerner is that he underwent flexor tendon surgery in October, an injury that wasn't made public until the season's conclusion. He may be ready for spring training, but the Cubs have been relatively vague on his recovery. However, it's expected to take about four months, and he should be ready to go when the season kicks off or shortly after that. This uncertainty leads to a buying opportunity, as Hoerner isn't going off the board until around pick 170 (2B10). While the pick doesn't come with some risk, getting a massive discount after the season he just had is something managers should strongly consider, especially at such a weak position.

4. **Jonathan India, KC (G: 133 2B, 18 DH):** India had a very solid 2024, the best season since he broke onto the scene as a rookie in 2021. Playing in 151 games, the 27-year-old had 15 HR, 84 R, 58 RBI, 13 SB, and a .248 batting average. The big variable in this equation is that India was dealt to the Royals in November, a drastic change of scenery for several reasons. Firstly, the ballpark. Overall, Great American Ballpark in Cincinnati and Kauffman Stadium in KC grade out reasonably similarly, as a 105 and 104 park factor, respectively. This encompasses the entire offensive environment for the two fields. The big difference is the HR factor, as GABP ranks 1st in baseball with a 128, whereas Kauffman ranks 4th last at 85. This means that India will likely give back a few HR this season, but his overall offensive production could increase as Kauffman is very friendly for hitting doubles and triples. India has excellent on-base skills (career .352 OBP), and leading off in front of Bobby Witt Jr will be appealing for fantasy purposes.

5. **Xander Bogaerts, SD (G: 85 2B, 20 SS, 9 DH):** Bogaerts had a down year in 2024, but we can attribute most of his struggles to a shoulder injury he suffered in May. If you look at his production in the second half, when he was presumably healed back up, Bogaerts hit .292 with 7 HR and 9 SB. Considering his early ADP of 156 (2B9), he feels like a steal. Steamer projects him at 17 HR/14 SB/.271, and considering the strength of the Padres' lineup around him, that could very easily come with 80+ runs and 80+ RBI. His SwStr% has been trending down for the past three seasons, and his power metrics have been relatively unchanged from prior seasons. A fully healthy Bogaerts (which he appears to be now) could be one of the better deals you find on the board all draft season, with easy Top 100 overall potential even as he enters his age 32 season. A bonus here is that you will also get the dual 2B/SS eligibility in all formats, as he was able to sneak in 20 games at short in 2024. It's hard to overstate the benefit of that added versatility when setting your lineups.

6. **Bryson Stott, PHI (G: 137 2B, 14 SS, 1 DH):** Stott had a bit of a down year but was still a serviceable option, finishing as the 2B13 overall. In 148 games, he contributed 11 HR, 65 R, 57 RBI, 32 SB, and a .245 batting average. After hitting .280 in 2023, the batting average dip is probably the most disappointing aspect of his season, but it's also worth noting that the difference in his xBA between the seasons was only nine points (.267 to .258). He's not an especially powerful man, but he should still be able to produce double-digit HR year in and year out based on his solid launch angle. His walk rate also jumped from 6.1% to 9.3%, meaning his OBP remained unchanged from 2023. Stott is locked into an everyday role in the middle of a fantastic lineup, and it seems like the market has over-corrected itself on his value. He's available as the 2B12, which is reasonable, but he's making it until pick 180 in most rooms, making him a relatively easy pick as a good bounce-back candidate.

7. **Gleyber Torres, DET (G: 153 2B):** Undoubtedly, Torres was one of the most disappointing fantasy assets in 2024, regardless of position. Coming into the season as a Top 100 pick in most rooms, Gleyber regressed in all five standard roto categories. In 154 games, he hit 15 HR with 80 R, 63 RBI, 4 SB, and a .257 batting average. He also lost a bit of juice on his barrel (7.9% to 6.3%) and HardHit rates (40.3% to 35.4%). That being said, things improved significantly for him in the second half as he hit .292 with 7 HR, so there is hope he figured things out as the season went along. There's also the report that he was playing through an undisclosed injury early in the season, so perhaps that was the genesis of his down year. Detroit should take some pressure off him and he's reasonably priced at 2B15 with an ADP of 188.

Red Flags

1. **Andrés Giménez, CLE (G: 152 2B):** After a breakout 2022 season that pushed him into the elite fantasy second base tier, there has been a downward trend of production for Andrés Giménez. Suiting up in 152 games, the 26-year-old managed just 9 HR, 64 R, 63 RBI, 30 SB, and a .252 batting average. Some of the trajectories are genuinely concerning. His barrel rate went from a mediocre 5.5% down to 2.8%, his OPS went from .712 to .638, and his wRC+ (141 in 2022) went from 96 down to 83. His exceptional defense will keep him on the field nearly every day, but that may not be good for those who draft him. The steals are about the only projectable positive in his fantasy game, and then you'd be praying that he can get his batting average back up into the .260/.270 range for him to be worth a spot on your team. With his sub .300 OBP, it's also hard to see him occupying a spot at the top of the Guardians' lineup. His 184 ADP isn't terrible if you desperately need the speed he provides, but he's not someone you should be targeting on draft day, given how his skills have been degrading lately.

2. **Nolan Gorman, STL (G: 105 2B, 2 3B):** Nolan Gorman is one of those players who could be great if a few tweaks were made, but that is much easier said than done. Playing in 107 games in 2024, the 24-year-old slugger hit 19 HR with 42 R, 50 RBI, 6 SB, and a .203 batting average. His profile is similar to many sluggers except more extreme than most. His 16.7% barrel rate is as elite as they come, but the downside is that he struck out 37.6% of the time with an 18.5% SwStr rate. It doesn't matter how much power you have if you strike out that much, and the Cardinals realized that as well, as he was optioned to AAA in August. He is a very streaky player who makes for a decent streaming option when he gets going, but he isn't someone that you should even think about drafting outside of very deep formats. He absolutely can turn things around; he still hasn't even turned 25, but he's far too risky to trust as a starting option in 2025.

Up and Coming

1. **Colt Keith, DET (G: 133 2B, 14 DH):** After struggling with his initial adjustment to big league pitching, Keith figured things out and became a solid option off the waiver wire down the stretch. He played 148 games and contributed 13 HR, 54 R, 61 RBI, 7 SB, and a .260 batting average in an impressive rookie campaign. Even though he struggled early on, he never looked overmatched at the plate. His 6.5 BB% and 19.8 K% are excellent for rookies, especially a 22-year-old. While his 5.6 barrel% and 35 hardhit% weren't impressive, he did underperform his xBA, xSLG, and xwOBA. The young stud will be locked into an everyday role once again, and you can't overstate the improvement in the Tigers lineup over the past couple of seasons. Keith is projected for across-the-board improvement by Steamer, and it's very easy to envision him taking another step forward this season in all categories. His 234 ADP (2B19) is a fantastic bargain for a player with his skillset and situation.

2. **Jackson Holliday, BAL (G: 56 2B, 3 SS, 1 DH):** Boy, was 2024 ever a year that Jackson Holliday would like to wipe from his memory. Entering the season as the #1 overall prospect in baseball with generational upside and a HOF-worthy father, expectations were understandably massive. Holliday made his major league debut on April 4th, was sent back down on April 23rd, and then recalled again at the end of July. He totaled 60 games at the big league level, hitting 5 HR with 28 R, 23 RBI, 4 SB, and a .189 batting average. Many were expecting Holliday to fare much better during his second stint, and while it was a slight improvement, he was still well below average as a hitter. All we can do is hope that this first year in the show provided Holliday with some key information on what he needs to do (and change) to succeed. He should be afforded the opportunity to play every day in a great lineup right out of the gate, and as a sophomore, that might be all it takes to get him going, but there is also a chance that his growing pains will linger into year two. His 217 ADP (2B17) certainly isn't cost-prohibitive for you to find out, either.

3. **Zack Gelof, ATH (G: 138 2B):** After a mesmerizing 69-game sample in 2023 that had him looking like a breakout star, Zack Gelof didn't quite live up to lofty expectations in 2024. Playing in 138 games, Gelof put up 17 HR, 60 R, 49 RBI, 25 SB, and a .211 batting average, finishing as the 2B21 overall on the season. The big trouble was his strikeout rate, which jumped from 27.3% to 34.4%. His walk rate also went from 8.7% to 6.9%, and his OBP was a horrible .270, primarily because of that. He also lost some power, going from an 11.1% barrel rate down to a solid 8.8%. However, Steamer is expecting him to bounce back in 2025. They are projecting 20 HR, 64 R, 64 RBI, 23 SB, and a .223 batting average. It's also worth noting that the Athletics will go from the pitcher-friendly Colosseum in Oakland to a much more hitter-friendly PCL park in Sacramento. Gelof (and the A's as a whole) should see an improvement in their offensive prowess as a unit and more counting stats could be there to go around their group of budding stars. Gelof is going around pick 225 as the 2B19, which seems like a perfectly reasonable price for the former 2nd-round draft pick.

4. **Spencer Horwitz, PIT (G: 41 1B, 39 2B):** Horwitz split time between second and first base for the Blue Jays, and the 26-year-old rookie did not disappoint. Playing in 97 games, he provided 12 HR, 46 R, 40 RBI, and a .265 batting average. This came with an excellent .790 OPS and 127 wRC+. Horowitz only struck out 18.4% of the time, and his superb 7.8 SwStr% suggests that should have been even a bit lower. He also walked 11% of the time, which helped lead to a .357 OBP. The power was also on display, as his 8% barrel rate and nearly 14-degree launch angle proved very effective at the dish. After spending many years bouncing around Toronto's farm system, it appears that Horwitz wasn't entirely a part of the Blue Jays' future after all. His price is incredibly reasonable, and he is currently not being selected until around pick 317 as the 27th second baseman off the board. With projections essentially expecting a repeat performance this coming season, he's a quality draft pick as your second baseman or middle infielder. He'll also come with first-base eligibility so that you can stick him into a corner infield spot. The value here could be immense.

Serviceable

1. **Brandon Lowe, TB (G: 58 2B, 37 DH, 13 1B):** Lowe did about what we were expecting coming into the season: He provided solid per-game production but had to miss time due to side, oblique, and toe injuries. Over 107 games, the 30-year-old hit 21 HR with 56 R, 58 RBI, 5 SB, and a .244 batting average. His 12.4% barrel rate significantly improved over the last two seasons, where he was around the 10% mark. His .229 ISO was also the best number he had put up since his 39 HR campaign in 2021. Lowe is very reasonably priced with an ADP of 244 (2B20). While he does have an extensive injury history, it is pretty random ailments that keep him out as opposed to the same lingering injury, which makes you feel better about his prospects of staying on the field. He's a nice late source of power who can chip in a few steals, and the Rays will also benefit from playing in a minor league park in 2025. He'll be one of my favorite mid-round targets of the season.

2. **Jeff McNeil, NYM (G: 110 2B, 28 OF):** McNeil had a disappointing season overall but did pick things up in the second half to make his overall line much more respectable. In 129 games, McNeil hit 12 HR (the 2nd highest total of his career) with 57 R, 44 RBI, 5 SB, and a .238 batting average. As a .289 career hitter, the low batting average was probably the most disappointing element of his season, but that doesn't mean McNeil can't still be an asset there going forward. His .256 BABIP was the lowest mark of his career, and Steamer projects that to rise back up to .295 this season, with a .271 batting average in turn. Considering that he is pretty locked into playing time in New York, he is one of the better late options to help out your batting average in a given draft room. He's also projected for another 12 HR and 134 R+RBI, so it seems like he will be a solid asset again in 2025. He's an excellent option for your bench, and his 451 ADP (2B41) is just far too low.

3. **Nick Gonzales, PIT (G: 85 2B, 8 SS, 2 3B):** Gonzales had his first true taste of being a big leaguer and did well with the opportunity. Over 94 games, he hit 7 HR to go along with 42 R, 49 RBI, 5 SB, and a .270 batting average. His major asset would be his 93rd-percentile sprint speed, suggesting he had the potential to steal quite a few more bases. He also displayed solid power with his 7.9% barrel rate and slightly underperformed almost all his expected stats. It is somewhat puzzling why he is going so late in drafts (375 ADP, 2B33). He projects as an everyday player in 2025 who won't hurt you in any of the five standard roto categories, and he is going later than almost all of the other starting caliber options at the position. He's a massive target at the moment, assuming that his price doesn't jump through the roof (which it shouldn't).

4. **Thairo Estrada, FA (G: 94 2B, 1 DH):** Thairo was one of the biggest fantasy disappointments of the 2024 season. He was viewed as a very safe option entering the season, a player who could assist in all five categories and potentially excel regarding stolen bases. A disaster ensued, as Estrada played just 96 games due to wrist and hamstring injuries and a demotion to Triple-A. He managed 9 HR, 43 R, 47 RBI, 2 SB, and a .217 batting average. Oddly, his profile didn't change much from previous seasons. His barrel and hard-hit rates stayed approximately the same, his groundball and flyball rates were about the same, and he even shaved a few points off his strikeout rate. So what happened? The BABIP gods played a significant role in his struggles, as Estrada's .249 mark was the lowest of his career. Steamer projects his BABIP at .289 with a .248 average, which would be welcome following the season he just had. Estrada is a free agent, and while his landing spot (and playing time) will indeed dictate some of his value, he is essentially free in drafts this season. His 478 ADP (2B42) makes it easy to buy back in at the end of your draft to see if he can rebound and become a solid fantasy contributor.

AL/NL Only

1. **Jorge Polanco, SEA (G: 112 2B, 5 DH):** 2024 was an absolute disaster for Polanco. He was traded to Seattle (one of the most pitcher-friendly parks in baseball) and did not fare well. Playing in 118 games, he hit just 16 HR with 43 R, 45 RBI, 4 SB, and a .213 batting average. His biggest issue was strikeouts, as his 29.2 K% and 11.8 SwStr% were by far the highest of his career. His barrel rate dropped from a robust 13.8% down to 8.9%, and his hard-hit rate also lost three points. It's hard to envision him landing a starting gig somewhere that would be a boon for fantasy, making Polanco more of a depth piece in most cases with his 431 ADP (2B 39).

2. **Brendan Rodgers, FA (G: 132 2B, 5 DH):** Rodgers became a free agent after being non-tendered by the Rockies in November. He played 135 games in 2024, hitting 13 HR with 67 R, 54 RBI, 1 SB, and a .267 batting average. It wasn't a terrible season, and he finished as the 2B19 overall on the year. The problem will be projecting a landing spot, as Rodgers benefited from hitter-friendly Coors Field, making his offensive contributions a bit of a question mark elsewhere. He's a risky play and should only be considered a depth piece on draft and hold/Only league squads.

3. **Gavin Lux, CIN (G: 138 2B, 1 SS):** After a few years of disappointing production, something clicked for Lux down the stretch. In the second half of the season (210 PA), Lux hit .304 with 7 HR and a .899 OPS. As a former first-round pick, he always had the pedigree, but most people lost hope before he went on his hot streak. The only potential problem here would be playing time, as the high-spending Dodgers could easily make a few moves this winter that relegates him to a bench role. Lux is now in a crowded infield mix in Cincinnati which is far from ideal.

4. **Brandon Drury, FA (G: 56 2B, 16 3B, 16 DH, 14 1B):** After two consecutive big seasons from Drury where he defied expectations, he came dramatically crashing back down to earth in 2024. Over 97 games with the Angels, Drury hit just 4 HR to go along with a miserable 28 R, 15 RBI, 1 SB, and a .169 batting average. He's now a 32-year-old free agent, and there's no real guarantee that he will latch on anywhere with a starting gig available. His 597 ADP (2B55) makes it easy to invest in a bounce-back if you are a believer, but it's hard to say he's a target of mine in any way.

5. **Michael Massey, KC (G: 82 2B, 14 DH):** Massey had himself a pretty serviceable season over the 100 games he played. He chipped in with 14 HR, 45 R, 45 RBI, 1 SB, and a .259 average. The Jonathan India trade could complicate his playing time situation. Still, there is also a good chance that India will assume a regular DH role, and Massey will stay at the keystone position. It likely doesn't help him overall, but if Massey ends up hitting fifth, as Roster Resource on FanGraphs currently suggests, he could end up being more than an AL Only option. However, the cautious drafter will avoid investing too much in Massey if India takes over 2B and Massey is left as a utility option.

6. **Edouard Julien, MIN (G: 90 2B, 3 DH, 1 1B):** Edouard Julien has the skillset to be a great fantasy asset, but some of his flaws are still pretty damning. He played 94 big league games in 2024, hitting 8 HR along with 36 R, 21 RBI, 6 SB, and a .199 batting average. The biggest problem is his strikeout rate, as Julien finished at 33.9 K%. His 11.5 SwStr% suggests that he could eventually get that down, but it has been a problem for him now in multiple seasons. He has excellent on-base skills and a solid power/speed mix, but the Twins won't give him the reins at 2B until he is fully ready, and we just aren't quite there yet.

7. **Otto López, MIA (G: 103 2B, 8 SS, 6 3B, 4 DH, 2 OF):** Otto López was one of the more valuable in-season pickups of 2024. Playing in 117 games, he hit .270 with 6 HR, 49 R, 39 RBI, and 20 SB. While immensely valuable, seeing him repeating those same heights in 2025 is tough. His wRC+ was just 91, implying that he was roughly 10% worse than the league average as a hitter overall. He doesn't have much power and has an awful lineup around him, which will limit his potential for counting stats. He's more of a speed specialist than anything else, but he does have a lot of potential, and it wouldn't shock me to see him much higher up on this list next season if things break right.

8. **Nicky Lopez, FA (G: 83 2B, 45 SS):** Nicky Lopez was not much of an asset in 2024 outside of incredibly deep formats. In 124 games, he hit just 1 HR with 40 R, 21 RBI, and 5 SB, with a .241 batting average. He's a free agent with no guarantee of a starting gig in 2025. He will likely become a bench bat or play a utility role going forward. Not at all someone to target.

9. **Enmanuel Valdéz, BOS (G: 65 2B, 4 DH, 1 OF):** Valdéz was very pedestrian in 2024. He hit .214 with 6 HR, 23 R, 28 RBI, and 1 SB. He likely won't have much of a role with the Red Sox in 2025. A bench bat/utility role is about as much as you should hope for, but he's not someone to look at, even in incredibly deep leagues.

Chapter 8

Third Basemen

	Leagues w/o CINF	RPV
1	Jose Ramirez	34%
2	Gunnar Henderson	22%
3	Vlad Guerrero	19%
4	Rafael Devers	17%
5	Jazz Chisholm	5%
6	Manny Machado	-1%
7	Austin Riley	-1%
8	Mark Vientos	-6%
9	Junior Caminnero	-6%
10	Alex Bregman	-7%
11	Royce Lewis	-9%
12	Jordan Westburg	-9%
13	Spencer Steer	-11%
14	Jake Burger	-13%
15	Matt Chapman	-15%
16	Nolan Arenado	-17%

	Leagues w/ CINF	RPV
1	Jose Ramirez	46%
2	Gunnar Henderson	33%
3	Vlad Guerrero	29%
4	Rafael Devers	27%
5	Jazz Chisholm	14%
6	Manny Machado	8%
7	Austin Riley	8%
8	Mark Vientos	2%
9	Junior Caminnero	2%
10	Alex Bregman	1%
11	Royce Lewis	-1%
12	Jordan Westburg	-1%
13	Spencer Steer	-3%
14	Jake Burger	-5%
15	Matt Chapman	-7%
16	Nolan Arenado	-10%
17	Alec Bohm	-10%
18	Isaac Paredes	-12%
19	Eugenio Suarez	-14%
20	Luis Rengifo	-16%
21	Yandy Diaz	-18%
22	Josh Jung	-24%
23	Matt Shaw	-25%
24	Coby Mayo	-26%

***Get updated RPV Cheat for one time $5 cost (free updates)
PayPal: FantasyBlackBook@gmail.com or Venmo: @FantasyBlackBook
And include your email address***

Third Baseman Profiles & Overview
By Chris Welsh

Third base, as a whole, might be the deepest infield position outside of shortstops. Looking at players that had at least 100 at-bats, 10 players hit 24 or more home runs, nine of which hit over .245 (Paul DeJong is the only outlier). Sixteen players stole 10 or more bases, while eight of those hit 10 or more home runs (using the 100 at-bats as a baseline).

Just six qualified third basemen are inside the early NFBC top 100, and just 15 are inside the top 200. Yet, the positional depth goes into the thirties of the position. Unlike some positions that carry the "top-heavy" tag, third base is more "Jose Ramirez" and then "middle-heavy." You have solid third basemen, about 12 deep. This allows you to cover a few other positions if you wish, hit third base later, and most likely find your corner infielder from third base as well.

Don't be surprised when third base is a position that, more often than not, beats ADP value by the end of the year. Don't get too cute, as you shouldn't pass on Jose Ramirez because it's deep, but it has more depth than first base currently looks.

The Elite

1. **Jose Ramirez, CLE (G: 126 3B):** Ramirez put up an elite-of-elite type of season. He led all third basemen in four of the five roto categories. He set career highs in runs at 114 and stolen bases at 41 and tied a career-high in home runs at 39. He added on top 118 RBI and a .279 average. He increased his barrel percentage to 8.6%, the highest since 2021. He hit an all-time high in his max exit velocity of 116.6mph. His .364 wOBA was in the top nine percentile of the league. He pairs these hitting skills with an almost 20-degree launch angle. This is important, as Cleveland changed their right field, creating a wind tunnel that helped left-handed hitters. In 2024, Cleveland had the fifth-best ballpark factor for left-handed hitters to hit home runs and the 7th best overall ballpark factor for left-handed hitters. The question for Ramirez is whether he can repeat it. The negatives start with his xBA, just .259, the third lowest of his career. His hard-hit numbers fell under 40%, and his walk rate fell to the second lowest of his career at just 7.9%, the first time under 10 in the last five years. Projections still have him as an elite hitter, but he is not quite repeating this massive production. Steamer has him hitting .279 with 31 home runs and 31 stolen bases. Even with his strikeouts creeping a bit up, walks creeping down, and chase rate rising to over 30% for the first time, he makes such quality contact and understands some of the new ballpark factors that it feels very safe to bank on a 30/30 season. Ramirez should go off the board in the top seven or eight draft picks.

Top Talent

1. **Austin Riley, ATL (G: 109 3B):** Riley had a lower statistical season due to an injury near the end of the year. He finished with a .256 average, 19 home runs, and the lowest run and RBI totals in a season where he had played at least 100 games. Even with the missed games, his power numbers ticked down a bit, yet his underlying stats were popping. He ranked in the 90th percentile of the league in xwOBA, xSLG, AVG EV, barrel percentage, hard-hit percentage, and bat speed. He improved his barrel percentage year over year and set career highs in average exit velocity at 93.3 mph and hard hit percentage at 53.4%. There were a few other areas of improvement as well that you would guess led to a better season. He improved his ground ball rate from 41.1% to 36.2% and his zone contact percentage from 79.1% to 81.3%. So, what brought Riley down? He struggled against lefties this year. He hit .275 or higher over the last three seasons, but in 2024, he hit just .235. The other glaring negative was his work against four-seam fastballs. In 2023, he hit .250 against four-seams, but that fell in 2024 to just .172. Four-seam fastballs were the number one pitch he saw at 35%. The positive is that his xBA on four-seam fastballs was .242, almost 15 points higher than the previous year. That speaks to positive regression when you consider his fantastic underlying metrics. Riley is going outside the top 30 in early drafts and is a great target if he falls into the third round.

2. **Rafael Devers, BOS (G: 130 3B):** Devers has become the prototype third baseman. He hit 28 home runs, now four straight years of 27 or more home runs in a season. He hit .272, now four consecutive seasons of hitting .271 or better. He also has an xBA of .272 or higher in four straight seasons. He had a great 13% barrel rate, slightly better than last season, and ranked in the 88th percentile. His 52% hard-hit rate ranked in the 95th percentile of the league, and is now four straight seasons of a 50% or higher percentage. His ability to make consistent hard contact speaks for itself. Still, even more impressively, he hit .260 or higher among the three pitch types of fastball, breaking, and offspeed, according to Baseball Savant. We saw a slight downtick in his pull percentage, which could have played a role in the slight power dip. His strikeout rate went up to 24.5%, the highest since 2020. He struggled against lefties this year. He had hit .270 or higher in the three previous seasons but fell to .240 in 2024. Devers also ended the year poorly. He hit 23 of his 28 home runs in the first half of the season with a .291 average. In the second half, just .244 with five home runs in about 100 less at-bats. His bat skills provide an incredible floor, and outside of injury, he might be the safest late second to early third-round pick there is. Steamer projections have him improving in four of the five major roto categories.

3. **Manny Machado, SDP (G: 100 3B):** There was a school of thought that Manny was starting a downward trend in his career. In 2024, he put up another solid year. He hit .275 with a .272 xBA, almost 20 points higher than the previous year. He hit 29 home runs, now four straight years of 28 or more. He also topped 100 RBI with 105, the third time in four years going over 100. Machado improved his hard-hit percentage from 45.9% to 48.8%. He improved his average exit velocity from 91 mph to 92.5 mph. Machado finished the year strong, hitting .286 to finish the year versus .267 in the first half. Machado did a lot of damage this year off of four-seamers and sinkers. He struggled against sliders, dropping almost 100 batting points against and nearly doubling his strikeout percentage to 26%. Pitchers threw more sinkers to him than fastballs, which was a change from 2023. Machado has a fast swing that came in at 75.3mph, which, on average, was in the 90th percentile of the league. More than half of his swings come in at 75mph or higher, double the league average. This makes up for a relatively longer swing, but if age catches up and he loses any speed on it, plus an uptick in sliders, Machado could run into some troubles. It's something to keep an eye on as he turns 33 in July. Besides the nits to pick, his baseline looks really good, and he produces similarly to Devers and Riley while going nearly a round later.

Solid Options

1. **Royce Lewis, MIN (G: 51 3B | 2 2B):** Lewis once again wasn't able to stay healthy, finishing just south of 300 at-bats on the year, but as he does, he put up big power numbers with 16 home runs over that period. While Lewis did maintain his above-average barreling and big launch angle, there were quite a few dips in his overall game. His average fell from over .300 to .233. His xBA was better but still sat at .246. As nice as the power numbers were, he hit nine of his 16 home runs in June. If yCombining other months played, theydoes equal nine home runs. The most concerning might be his hard-hit percentage dip. After putting up a 42% hard-hit rate, it fell to 37% this past year. He lost three MPH of exit velocity against fastballs while losing over 130 batting points. He also struggled mightily against changeups from a batting average and exit velocity standpoint. All of this combined with him hitting just .207 in the second half, which accounted for most of his season at-bats. He comes with a more significant injury risk than most, but if he can stay healthy, he's probably a good bet for a 30-home-run season. He may be trending as a lower batting average hitter, though, somewhere between .240-.260. His ADP is favorable at just around 100 overall.

2. **Mark Vientos, NYM (G: 108 3B | 4 1B):** Vientos' production and underlying stats tell us the story of one of the next big power hitters in the game. It took just over 400 at-bats for Vientos to put up 27 home runs to go with a .266 batting average and 71 RBI. His .246 xBA supports the average range that he is in. This goes well with those power numbers. He had a 14.1% barrel percentage, which was in the 91st percentile of the league. This went with an 11.4-degree launch angle and a 46.1% hard-hit rate. The batted ball speaks very well to future big home runs, but he did have one of the bigger home runs to xHR differentials, with six fewer home runs on the expected side. He has a big strikeout problem, as it sits at 29.7% of the time. He's a heavy fastball hitter. That can sometimes be a worry, as the league could then adjust, but he is one of the few players who saw sliders more than any other pitch. He didn't fare well but still dominated. This could give a little ease to those worried that the league will make a big adjustment on him because they already have. Ironically, his 2024 teammate Pete Alonso might be a good representation of who he could be. He is going right in front of Royce Lewis in early drafts and a fair cost for 30-plus projected home runs.

3. **Jordan Westburg, BAL (G: 67 3B | 53 2B | 2 SS):** Westburg settled into third base as the team moved Holliday in as their second baseman. He hit .264 with 18 home runs, 67 RBI, and six stolen bases in 107 games. Westburg's xBA was .281, which ranked inside the 92nd percentile of the league. His batted ball skills are well above average with an 11.8% barrel percentage, a 46.1% hard-hit rate, and an over 13-degree launch angle. While hitting the ball with authority, he dropped his strike-out percentage from 24% to 21%. Westburg's 30% chase rate is a bit high, and he has an average to below-average zone contact rate, which we want to improve. He did have a dramatic home/road split, hitting over .300 at home and just .220 on the road. His home environment, though, will get friendly for him as they are shortening the right field deck for pull-side home runs. Steamer projections see him going 20/10 with a .260 average. His underlying stats show a player that could beat projections across the board.

4. **Junior Caminero, TB (G: 39 3B | 1 1B):** Before being called to the majors, Caminero hit 16 home runs in just 59 minor league games. The 21-year-old showed similar quality of contact skills in the majors, posting a 11.8% barrel percentage and a 45.7% hard hit rate. He hit a max exit velocity of 116.3 mph, which ranked him in the 98th percentile of the league. His 77.2 mph bat speed would have registered as one of the fastest in the league but also one of the longest at 8.3 feet. Caminero is not a strikeout guy at 21% but posted a 35% chase rate, which is far above average. Early projections are favorable for Caminero to hit between 25-30 home runs with a .260 batting average. There could be some rookie adjustment as teams adjust to pitching him with his long swing and chase rate, but he has shown a knack for adapting to levels. He is going off the board just outside the top 100 clump of third baseman.

5. **Alex Bregman, FA (G: 142 3B):** Even though everyone has dreamed of Bregman's 2019 season, he has at least become a model of consistency in the past three years. He's hit between .259 and .262 and 23 to 26 home runs over the last three seasons. He's a quality contact hitter, not a big impact hitter. He raised his barrel percentage from 5.4% to 6.4%, jumped from 38.4% hard hit to 40.5%, and had an xBA close to his average of .256. His zone contact percentage sits at an elite 91.3%. His high contact percentage and his low strikeout rates create a great floor as a fantasy player. He hit 16 of his 26 home runs in 2024 in Houston, so his 2025 team could play a role in his home run production if he goes to a pitcher-friendly environment. With an early NFBC ADP outside the top 140, Bregman might be a steal at the position in 2025.

6. **Matt Chapman, SF (G: 154 3B):** Chapman bounced back from a down 2023 with 27 home runs, which he's done now in three of the last four years, along with a .240 average, 98 runs, and a career-high 15 stolen bases. In fact, he stole more bases in 2024 than his entire career combined. Chapman saw a five percent decline in his barrel percentage, hard-hit percentage by six percent, and a few degrees off his launch angle. He also put up one of the best average exit velocities at 93.2 mph. Despite the declines, his numbers were still above average, putting up a .250 xBA,, the highest since 2019, and an 81.1% zone contact rate,, almost 10 percent higher than the previous year. One significant change from Chapman was his approach to sliders. He had a better average, lower WHIFF rate, and strikeout rate. Steamer projections see a mostly repeat from 2023, making his post 125 ADP look like a bit of a deal.

Red Flags

1. **Nolan Arenado, STL (G: 154 3B):** Other than his rookie year, 2024 was the most disappointing season to date for Arenado. He hit 16 home runs with 71 RBI and 70 runs, all three of which have now been on a four-year decline. He had a .272 average with a .250 xBA, which was doable, but this comes with a 3.2% barrel percentage and a 31.6% hard-hit rate, both of which were dramatic drop-offs from the previous season. Arenado hit a career-low average exit velocity of 86.3 mph, one of the worst in the league. He hit .295 against fastballs, which was the best in years, but hit an all-time low exit velocity against at 87.8 mph, which accounted for most of his overall dip. Overall, he made better contact, but with less hard-hit skills, everything became mediocre. This may be the start, or we may be in the middle of the scary age decline. Projections see a home run bounce back, but his ADP is outside the top 200.

2. **Alec Bohm, PHI (G: 128 3B | 15 1B):** Bohm hit .280 with 15 home runs and 97 RBI. When you look at his profile, it's almost mystifying that he hasn't put up a bigger season. His xBA was even higher at .288, a 45.6% hard-hit rate was a 4% jump year over year, and at least league average max exit velocity and average exit velocity. It may start with the ability not just to put wood on the bat, but barrels. He has just a 6.8% barrel rate. His 10-degree launch angle could do more if the contact quality were higher. His high average and low strikeouts, which were just 14% this year,, speak very well to points leagues. But currently, he isn't much more than a two-plus category player. There have been trade rumors for Bohm. He hit .306 on the road vs. home this past year, so the right destination could unlock some untapped potential. At the end of the day, though, he has never been a massive analytics tweak type of player, so if the barrels don't go up, he may struggle to put up more than 20 home runs. His early ADP has him going outside the top 150.

3. **Josh Jung, TEX (G: 40 3B):** Jung only got 46 games in due to injuries in 2024. He hit .264 and seven home runs. He saw some steep declines in his underlying stats with a 9.9% barrel rate, which was two percent less year over year, an 86.2% average exit velocity, which was almost five mph less, and an almost 10 percent hard hit percentage drop down to 39.7%. He lowered his strikeout percentage from 29% to 25%, but his swing and miss is still a big problem combined with an under-five percent walk rate. His zone contact percentage dropped three percent while putting up an over 35% chase rate. The drop in contact quality shines a concerning light on his ceiling, while lingering injury issues are also present in his young career. He's being drafted outside the top 200 but is in a range of options that might still be better.

Serviceable

1. **Eugenio Suarez, ARI (G: 155 3B):** There was a point in this where Eugenio was close to being cut by the Dbacks as he hit just .216, but absolutely shoved in the second half by hitting .307 with 20 home runs. He finished the year hitting .256 with 30 home runs and 101 RBI, the third highest among all third basemen. He put up the best xBA since 2019 at .247, which is key for him to hit above that .240 mark so he can tap into his immense power. He had an 11.3% barrel percentage with a 42% hard-hit rate while lowering his K% to 27%. He had been 29% or higher the previous four seasons. If he continues this path of lower Ks, the Dbacks seem committed to him, and their offense creates many run opportunities in front of him to continue that RBI pace. Projections are quite a bit lower but do pull from a three-year window. It's essential to note Arizona has the sixth-best ballpark factor for right-handed hitters. He's going as the 15th third baseman in early NFBC ADPs.

2. **Luis Rengifo, LAA (G: 48 3B | 31 2B | 2 SS | 1 OF):** Rengifo hit .300 with six home runs and a career-high 24 stolen bases before hurting himself on a swing in August and then rupturing a tendon in his bicep in August. Rengifo tanked his barrel percentage, falling from 7.6% to 2.5%, but this also correlated with him hitting for a much higher average and a career-high xBA of .262. He has two different swings. From the right side, it's a slower, more compact swing, which he hit over .350 against lefties. His swing gets faster and longer from the left side, where most of his power seems to be. His swing percentage went up, as did his zone contact percentage. He's a great combination of potential power, impact stolen bases, and multi-position eligibility. He had hit 16 and 17 home runs the prior two years, so projections are not considering some of the new potential adjustments he may be making. Those Steamer projections, though, are massive, with him at 17 home runs, 23 stolen bases, and a .263 average. If you buy into this, his post-170 ADP is a huge steal.

3. **Maikel Garcia, KC (G: 124 3B | 37 2B | 4 SS | 1 OF):** Garcia hit just .231 after hitting .272 in 2023. His home run total jumped a little year over year from four to seven, but he set career highs with 84 runs and 37 stolen bases. In 2023, Garcia posted an eye-popping 50% hard-hit rate, probably contributing to a relatively high .344 BABIP. Hiss hard-hit rate dropped to 42 this season%, and his BABIP crashed to .268. He lowered his strikeout rate dramatically, which might also be due to his understanding of the zone. While still posting respectable hard-hit numbers, I think that BABIP could have him being unlucky. He had a 50 higher xBA versus fastball than he hit, which also speaks to positive regression. He primarily hit out of the leadoff spot, which speaks well to his high run and stolen base numbers. He ranked second among third basemen in stolen bases and seventh overall. He'll have some multipositional eligibility, which will help his value. If you are prioritizing stolen bases or in a league that does so, he is an excellent bet, around 200 overall in drafts, assuming he can improve his average.

4. **Max Muncy, LAD (G: 72 3B):** Muncy played just 73 games but hit 15 home runs and a three-year best .232 average. Muncy is a dead-red fastball hitter, hitting .270 or higher against four-seam fastballs and sinkers but under .230 against all other pitch types. He has tremendous zone control with one of the league's lowest chase rates, an over 15% walk rate and a 26.3% strikeout rate. He has one of the most extreme launch angles at 26 degrees, so his game is to barrel fastballs, but year after year, he is a batting-average liability. He gets a boost in OBP leagues, but regardless of the 25-plus home run yearly projection, he simply is a three-category player with home runs, RBI, and runs and hurting your stolen bases and average. He'll be more of a corner infielder in fantasy if you are chasing power. NFBC drafts have him going outside the top 220.

5. **Ryan McMahon, COL (G: 152 3B):** McMahon is the model of consistency. In 2024, he hit .242 with 20 home runs, 65 RB, and 68 runs. He's now hit between .240 and .246 and an xBA between .243 and .247 in four straight years. He's hit between 20 and 23 home runs over that period. He even has within a handful of the same run, RBI, and stolen bases over the last four years. McMahon had career highs in his hard hit percentage at 49.7% and an average exit velocity at 92.1%. McMahon could have had a much bigger year if he didn't fall off the cliff. He hit .272 in the first half with 14 of his 20 home runs. He dropped to .188 in the second half and failed to hit over .232 from July on. McMahon's strikeout rate is still too high despite dropping by three percent, it was still 28%. He combats that with an over 10 percent walk rate, but he needs to make more contact as he has a 10.9% barrel rate but only a 66% zone swing rate. A player like McMahon gets an extra boost hitting Colorado. His projections are precisely what you'd expect from my writing here, but he is almost free, going past pick 250 in drafts.

6. **Isaac Paredes, HOU (G: 128 3B | 17 1B):** Paredes finished the year hitting .238 with 19 home runs. On the Rays, he was pacing out to have another solid power season with 16 home runs in just over 100 games with the Rays. Paredes was traded to the Cubs, where he hit .223 in just under 200 at-bats but hit just three home runs. Paredes is a low barrel (4.5%) and hard-hit (27.1%) batter but put up a monstrous 22.4-degree launch angle, which helped him make up for the low underlying data. This was a benefit with the Rays as he's an extreme pull hitter who gets the ball in the air, but the dimensions in Chicago don't work well for this. He's almost nothing with stolen bases and isn't much of a support with runs. Steamer projections have him at 24 home runs and a .240 average, but that might be optimistic. Although the Houstin ballpark in theory could push his home run total further.

AL/NL Only

1. **Connor Norby, MIA (G: 30 3B | 12 2B):** Norby, between the Orioles and Marlins, hit .236 with nine home runs and stole three bases. He had an elite 14.1% barrel rate paired with a 17-degree launch angle but had below-average hard-hit numbers. He's striking out too much at 33% of the time and needs to make more impact contact. He's projected on Steamer close to a 20 home run, 10 stolen base, and .240 plus season.

2. **Noelvi Marte, CIN (G: 55 3B | 1 2B):** Marte, in 66 games, hit .210 with four home runs and stole nine bases. He failed to hit over .230 in three of the four months he played. His strikeouts are a problem, as he struck out 31% of the time while putting up mediocre underlying metrics. Great American Ball Park boosts everyone's offense, but he'll have to continue to earn playing time—projections on a full season push 15/20, but with a poor average.

3. **Christopher Morel, TB (G: 74 3B | 21 2B | 11 OF):** Morel hit 21 home runs and eight stolen bases but just .196. Morel's barrel and hard hit rates went down, contributing to very little positive regression in his expected average with a .225 xBA. He got worse once he was traded to the Rays, failing to hit over .200 in the two months he was with the team. He has a little position flexibility but not much more than a 20/10 high projection with a poor average.

4. **Jeimer Candelario, CIN (G: 34 3B | 32 1B):** Candelario struggled with his average, hitting just .225 with a .221 xBA. He hit 20 home runs but lost some hard-hit metrics. He destroyed right-handed hitters, with 17 of his 20 coming off righties. He could go into a platoon, as the Reds have many options. The ballpark is always a boost. Projections have his average bouncing back up to .240 with 20-plus home runs.

Chapter 9

Shortstops

	Leagues w/o MINF	RPV
1	Mookie Betts	29%
2	Bobby Witt	25%
3	Gunnar Henderson	15%
4	Francisco Lindor	13%
5	Elly De La Cruz	12%
6	Willy Adames	0%
7	Corey Seager	-1%
8	Jackson Merrill	-1%
9	Trea Turner	-5%
10	O'Neill Cruz	-9%
11	C.J. Abrams	-12%
12	Matt McLain	-13%
13	Ezequiel Tovar	-13%
14	Bo Bichette	-15%
15	Brice Turang	-15%
16	Xander Bogaerts	-15%

	Leagues w/ MINF	RPV
1	Mookie Betts	40%
2	Bobby Witt	36%
3	Gunnar Henderson	25%
4	Francisco Lindor	23%
5	Elly De La Cruz	22%
6	Willy Adames	9%
7	Corey Seager	8%
8	Jackson Merrill	8%
9	Trea Turner	3%
10	O'Neill Cruz	-1%
11	C.J. Abrams	-4%
12	Matt McLain	-5%
13	Ezequiel Tovar	-5%
14	Bo Bichette	-7%
15	Brice Turang	-7%
16	Xander Bogaerts	-7%
17	Nico Hoerner	-9%
18	Anthony Volpe	-12%
19	Masyn Winn	-13%
20	Bryson Stott	-14%
21	Zach Neto	-19%
22	Maikel Garcia	-20%
23	Dansby Swanson	-25%
24	Carlos Correa	-25%

***Get updated RPV Cheat for one time $5 cost (free updates)
PayPal: FantasyBlackBook@gmail.com or Venmo: @FantasyBlackBook
And include your email address***

Shortstop Profiles & Overview
by Joe Orrico

As is usually the case, shortstop is among the deepest positions in fantasy baseball. According to early ADP data from the NFBC, the Top 10 shortstops are all going inside the Top 65 overall picks, and four of those names are in the first round. The following 11 shortstops are all going inside the Top 200 picks, so it is crucial to nail down one (if not two) of those elite names early on in your draft.

Considering the talent at the top of the board, I think it's best to secure one of the top six names (Witt, De La Cruz, Henderson, Betts, Lindor, or Turner) and then speculate on another option down the board to fill in your middle infield, utility, and/or bench spots.

A common misconception is that just because the position is deep, you should wait until the later rounds to draft your shortstop. However, it's very hard to replicate that surefire, five-category talent as the draft goes on. While there are some talented players available in the middle rounds, nabbing a top-tier shortstop is a big advantage when constructing your teams.

The Elite

1. **Bobby Witt Jr, KC (G: 160 SS, 1 DH):** Witt was a force to be reckoned with in 2024, taking another significant step forward after his breakout 2023 campaign. He put together a season that would have made him the easy choice for AL MVP in most seasons. Finishing with 32 HR, 125 R, 109 RBI, 31 SB, a .332 batting average, and 10.4 fWAR, Witt will be a very common choice as the 1.01 pick in 2025 drafts. It wasn't just his surface stats that improved, either. When you start digging, you will see massive jumps across the board. He raised his walk rate from 5.8% to 8% while dropping his strikeout rate from 17.4% to 15%. His barrel% went from 11.5% to 14.3%, and his hard-hit rate jumped from 45.4% to 48.1%. He had steady, consistent improvement across the board, fully backed up by every important metric we pay attention to. The counting stats haven't suffered even without another true star in the Kansas City lineup next to him. He is a self-sustaining asset that is leaps and bounds ahead of every other shortstop on the board.

2. **Mookie Betts, LAD (G: 65 SS, 43 OF, 18 2B):** Mookie had a very interesting season in 2024. He played shortstop as his primary position for the first time in his career while also spending time at second base and right field. He also missed almost 50 games recovering from a broken hand in August. And yet, he was still a phenomenal offensive force and fantasy asset. Over 116 games, he finished with 19 HR, 75 R, 75 RBI, 16 SB, and a .289 batting average. Consistency. That is the best word you can use to describe Mookie Betts. He has put up a WRC+ of at least 131 every year dating back to 2018, and he also has the luxury of being sandwiched between Shohei Ohtani and Freddie Freeman in the electric Dodgers' lineup. Even heading into his age 32 season, Mookie is one of the best offensive players in the game, and you get the luxury of an SS/OF designation (and maybe even 2B, depending on which site you play on). The missed games will lead to a slight discount in 2025 draft rooms, and you should be very interested in buying the dip.

3. **Gunnar Henderson, BAL (G: 157 SS, 2 DH):** Gunnar took a massive step forward overall, even if he did come back down to earth in the second half. His final output of 37 HR, 118 R, 92 RBI, 21 SB, and a .281 was good enough for a #7 overall finish on the FanGraphs player rater. Similarly to Bobby Witt Jr, the 23-year-old Henderson equaled or bettered his 2024 statistics across the board. When looking forward, we can expect things to get even better. Steamer has him projected at a 150 wRC+, which ranks sixth among all batters. They are forecasting 34 HR/18 SB/.275. With the improvements in the Orioles lineup over the past two seasons, it's very reasonable to expect Gunnar to reach (or eclipse) his projected 107 R and 91 RBI. The sky is the limit here, and he should easily return first-round value in 2025. He is well worth drafting as the foundational piece of your team in the middle of round one.

4. **Elly De La Cruz, CIN (G: 160 SS):** After the rumors that he could potentially be sent down to Triple-A if he struggled, Elly De La Cruz silenced his critics and emerged as one of the best and most exciting players the league offers. He stole a league-leading 67 bases while contributing 25 HR, 105 R, 76 RBI, and a much better-than-expected .259 batting average. No one doubted his raw power, but how it would translate to in-game success was another question altogether after he hit just 13 HR over 98 games as a rookie. However, EDLC raised his launch angle from 3.6° to 9.7° and raised his barrel rate by more than 4%, from 8.5 to a robust 12.7%. While some questions remain about his overall fantasy output (specifically with the RBI and batting average), Elly provides a massive cushion in SB that essentially guarantees a win in the category. He is more than capable of hitting 30+ HR, and the Reds will be getting some key pieces back into their lineup next season. While he doesn't provide the safety net of other players going around him in the first round, his ceiling is arguably as high as any player on the board.

5. **Francisco Lindor, NYM (G: 151 SS, 1 DH):** At age 30, Francisco Lindor has been a superstar for about eight years. He may have very well just painted his Mona Lisa in 2024. Playing in 152 games, he hit 33 HR (his fifth time surpassing 30) with 107 R, 91 RBI, 29 SB, and a .273 batting average. If it weren't for the otherworldly year that Shohei Ohtani had, Lindor would be putting an MVP trophy on his mantle this winter. He reached a new level offensively, crushing his previous highs in both barrel rate (13.4%) and hard-hit rate (47.4%). The crazy thing is he actually may have underperformed. His xBA, xSLG, and xWOBA were all higher than his actual totals, suggesting Lindor could have been even better in 2024 with more luck. While the supporting cast around him does leave something to be desired, he is still one of the elite contributors across the fantasy landscape, and he makes for a great wheel pick at the turn of Rounds 1 and 2. Everyone likes to shoot for upside, but there is something to be said for drafting a guy like Lindor and knowing precisely what you are going to get.

Top Talent

1. **Trea Turner, PHI (G: 118 SS, 3 DH):** Turner missed some time with a hamstring injury mid-season, but Trea Turner still had a very impressive campaign. He wasn't quite as productive once he returned, but he still finished the year with 21 HR, 88 R, 62 RBI, 19 SB, and a .295 batting average in 121 contests. We saw some slight decline in his power metrics (the barrel rate went from 8.4% to 6.9%) but nothing to be overly concerned about in the coming year. His 124 wRC+, .807 OPS, and .349 wOBA were all improvements from his 2023 marks. In an imposing Phillies lineup, Turner should still be a robust and four-category contributor going forward. He will enter the season healthy and likely be a Top 25 overall fantasy asset again.

2. **Corey Seager, TEX (G: 113 SS, 10 DH):** Despite dealing with hamstring, wrist, and hip issues throughout the season, Seager was still very productive in 2024. He hit the 30 HR plateau again despite playing in just 123 games. While he did take a bit of a step back offensively, going from a 171 wRC+ down to 140 isn't much of a concern to me. What is a bit of a concern, however, are the myriad health issues that seem to plague Seager every season. Drafting him should come with expectations of about 120 games, but that shouldn't scare you off. While many members of the Rangers took a step back in 2024, that is likely due to the deep playoff run to the World Series the previous season, and it almost certainly isn't something that will linger into next year. It's hard to find a better option than Seager on a per-game basis. He is in the 90th percentile or better in xwOBA, xBA, xSLG, avg exit velo, hard hit%, and barrel%. He is about as elite as they come; just remember that you will likely need to find a replacement for 1/4 of the season, and you'll be good to go.

Solid Options

1. **Oneil Cruz, PIT (G: 112 SS, 23 OF, 7 DH):** As much as I'd like to include Cruz in a higher tier, he hasn't earned that distinction yet. Don't get me wrong, he just put together a really solid year, but he hasn't entirely broken out in the way many have hoped. He played in 146 games this past season, which is by far a career high, and he produced 21 HR, 72 R, 76 RBI, and 22 SB while hitting .259. As the tier indicates, he is solid but not anything to write home about. While Cruz possesses massive power (15.7% barrel rate, 54.9% HardHit rate), his 9.8-degree launch angle isn't leading to as many HR as we would like. His 30.2 K%, backed up by a 15.1 SwStr%, is still a significant concern and could lead to years where his batting average is genuinely doing you a disservice. As his run and RBI totals indicate, he isn't playing in a great lineup in Pittsburgh. The raw talent is there for Cruz to put it all together and become a legitimate superstar, but until we see that come to fruition, he'll have to be considered a fine, but not outstanding, option at short.

2. **Bo Bichette, TOR (G: 81 SS):** Last season was a year to forget for Bo Bichette. He dealt with injuries to his neck, forearm, finger, and multiple to his calf, which kept him out for exactly half of the season. The 81 games he did play left a lot to be desired. Bo managed just 4 HR, 29 R, 31 RBI, 5 SB, and a .225 batting average for the miserable Blue Jays. His wRC+ was 71, and his OPS of .598 is even more startling. His barrel rate also fell dramatically from 9.6% down to 4.4%. Despite all this, it's hard to be genuinely concerned about Bichette. Between 2021-2023, only Freddie Freeman and Trea Turner had more base hits. Bo consistently gave us a 120 wRC+, 190 hits, and 20+ HR with excellent counting stats. One injury-plagued season at age 26 shouldn't impact our long-term outlook, yet we see massive discounts in the early 2025 draft room. The one-time 2nd/3rd round pick has now plummeted outside the Top 150 overall. There is a massive buy-back opportunity here, and drafters should eagerly await the opportunity to select him at such a discounted price.

3. **Willy Adames, SF (G: 161 SS):** Adames had a monster 2024 season, setting career highs nearly across the board. He played in 161 games and gave his managers 32 HR, 93 R, 112 RBI, 21 SB, and a .251 average. It's not too shabby for someone routinely going outside the Top 200 picks a season ago. The troubling part of the equation here is that Adames essentially had the same season as he did in 2023, at least when you look under the hood. His barrel, hard hit, xBA, xSLG, xwOBA, K%, BB%, and many other metrics remained unchanged between 2023 and 2024. The 21 SB are also hard to buy into, as Adames' sprint speed has been declining steadily for the last several years. While he doesn't quite make the cut for the "Red Flag" tier, he is someone to be careful with as you head into your drafts. His early ADP hovers around 60, which is very early for someone with his skillset in a loaded position. Hopefully, that price will come down, but if it stays where it currently is, he'd be someone to avoid at cost generally. Now, that's not to say that he will be bad or even a disappointment; he is just slightly out of my price range, considering his new home is unkind to right handed power.

4. **Zach Neto, LAA (G: 155 SS):** The 23-year-old Neto indeed had a breakout fantasy season in 2024, his first full year in The Show. Over 155 games, he had 23 HR, 70 R, 77 RBI, and 30 SB while batting .249, and having Ron Washington take over as his manager helped out on the basepaths. His sprint speed was relatively unchanged from 2023 when he stole just five bases in 84 games. Interestingly, most of his supporting metrics look very similar to 2023, so it is hard to pinpoint what led to his breakout. Still, we can attribute much of it to natural growth and progression, along with more comfortability after getting his feet wet last season. Now, a complicating factor is that Neto underwent shoulder surgery in early November, potentially delaying his season. This shouldn't totally scare you off of him, but it will still be a bit of a gamble to use an early draft pick on him, considering the depth available at the position. You also have to consider that the Angels' lineup around him will be a bit of a mess. You could argue that he is a red flag, but I think he's still a solid option assuming his price drops accordingly with the news of his surgery.

Red Flags

1. **CJ Abrams, WAS (G: 136 SS):** After starting the year on fire, Abrams came back down to earth and ended up having a fairly average season considering the expectations and elevated draft price heading into 2024. He played 138 games and finished with 20 HR, 79 R, 65 RBI, 31 SB, and a .246 batting average. In the second half of the season, Abrams hit .203 with just 5 HR. Another warning sign is that he was sent down to Triple-A to end the season after staying out all night at a casino on a game day. Perhaps he would be more appealing if he came at a discount this season, but his early ADP of 46 suggests that you will have to pay a pretty penny for him once again, and it just doesn't seem worth it. The only category he excels in is SB, a stat widely available throughout most draft rounds. There's still a bit of a misconception that you need to take speed guys early, which is why Abrams is still so expensive, but it should be less of a priority given the massive influx of SB over the past two seasons. He doesn't hit the ball terribly hard and has a suspect lineup around him, making Abrams an easy fade for me in the fourth round of drafts.

2. **Ezequiel Tovar, COL (G: 157 SS):** Tovar saw big improvement in 2024. He played 157 games and took home the gold glove for shortstops in the National League. According to FanGraphs, he finished as the SS8 overall and was an asset across all five categories. Tovar ended the season with 26 HR, 83 R, 78 RBI, 6 SB, and a .269 batting average. This was all great, but having confidence in him for 2025 is also a bit tough. First, his wRC+ of 95 suggests he is a below-league-average hitter. While his average was very good, his 3.3 BB% led to just a .295 OBP. His 28.8% strikeout rate is already very high, but his 19.2 SwStr% would suggest that he could easily strike out more than 30% of the time going forward. He also has a lousy lineup around him, and starting him when he is away from Coors won't be nearly as appealing as when he is at home. While his 71st percentile sprint speed is good, he stole just six bases on 11 attempts, so to expect more than maybe 10 next season would be a bit ambitious. As you can see, there are a lot of potential problems with his elevated draft cost (117) at such a deep position.

3. **Carlos Correa, MIN (G: 84 SS, 1 DH):** Correa was very good in 2024 on a per-game basis. He played 86 games and gave us 14 HR, 55 R, 54 RBI, and a .310 batting average. Now, why did he only play 86 games? Correa once again dealt with several injuries, including his wrist, hand, and foot, among others. This has been a common theme for many years now with Correa: solid production that just doesn't come with enough volume, and that problem isn't likely to get better now that he is on the wrong side of 30. You also have to consider that he isn't going to steal at all. His batting average is a massive variable year-to-year, and the Twins' lineup, while good in 2024, isn't guaranteed to repeat those same heights in 2025. While he is going for a reasonably significant discount in early drafts, he's not someone you should be planning to draft as a starting SS. If you end up with him, it means you missed out on the plethora of talent available in the earlier rounds, and it's likely to be a hole that needs constant filling on your roster.

Up and Coming

1. **Masyn Winn, STL (G: 148 SS, 1 DH):** Winn put together a great rookie season that would warrant ROY consideration in most normal seasons. As a finalist for the gold glove at SS, Winn provided fantasy managers with 15 HR, 85 R, 57 RBI, 11 SB, and a .267 batting average while serving as the Cardinals' primary leadoff hitter. He was in the .280s until a September slump dropped his batting average, but he does project to be an asset in the category going forward. His sprint speed is around the 90th percentile, which also bodes well for his SB potential. While his 3.2% barrel rate doesn't suggest much power, Steamer has him projected for 18 HR in 2025, partly due to his solid 13.2-degree launch angle. He's an excellent floor player, someone who won't hurt you in any category, and one of the latest sources of batting average available in a given draft. There's also an excellent chance that he spends the entire year in the leadoff spot, a role he only assumed part-way through 2024. While he might serve better as an MI option than your starting shortstop, he's still well worth his 180 ADP.

2. **Tyler Fitzgerald, SF (G: 72 SS, 11 OF, 6 2B, 3 DH, 2 1B):** Fitzgerald burst onto the scene in 2024 as a bit of a late bloomer at age 26 and subsequently became a league winner for those who took a chance and added him. Over 96 games and just over 300 AB, he had 15 HR, 53 R, 34 RBI, and 17 SB while hitting .280. His profile is a mixed bag when you look under the hood. Let's start with the good. Hitting the ground running like he did as a rookie is a positive sign going forward. His 8.2% barrel rate is solid, and he is one of the absolute fastest players in the league with his 100th-percentile sprint speed. Given how he played down the stretch, he will absolutely be given a shot as the starting shortstop entering 2025 without a ton of stiff competition for the role behind him. Now, for the ugly. Fitzgerald struck out 31.7% of the time, and his 13.9 SwStr% suggests that he will likely remain in the 28-30% range. While he barrels the ball up at a decent rate, his hard-hit percentage (31.4%) puts him in the 13th percentile. As someone without much prospect hype and pedigree behind him, it's tricky to know how to value him in 2025. That being said, his price is far lower than expected with an early ADP of 235 (SS23), and it isn't at all a cost-prohibitive draft pick in the later rounds to see if he can replicate his impressive showing as a rookie.

3. **Xavier Edwards, MIA (G: 69 SS):** The Marlins were mostly a disaster in 2024, but one of the lone bright spots was Xavier Edwards, and fantasy managers who added him were over the moon. He played in 70 games, and while he managed just one home run, he had 39 R, 26 RBI, 31 SB, and a robust .328 batting average. He displayed excellent plate skills considering his age and experience, putting up an excellent 10.9 BB% with a very respectable 17.2 K%. Power will never be a big part of his game with his 1.8% barrel rate and 23.9% hard hit, but that doesn't mean you shouldn't be interested in him. Steamer projects him to have 80 R and 35 SB while hitting .280, which will definitely play in most leagues. While the Marlins lineup isn't likely to do him many favors, Edwards can be a self-sustaining asset considering the categories you are counting on him for. His ADP of 175 (SS17) feels very reasonable, and he will be a great selection for those who prioritize power and decide to forego speed in the early rounds.

Serviceable

1. **Dansby Swanson, CHC (G: 148 SS):** Swanson took a step back in 2024 but was still a relatively productive fantasy asset. He played in 149 games and contributed 16 HR, 82 R, 66 RBI, 19 SB, and a .242 batting average. His barrel rate dropped by 1.7% and fell into the single digits for the first time since 2019, but his hard-hit rate increased from 39.5% to 42.5%. His expected stats were in line with his actual results, and it doesn't seem like luck was a major factor one way or the other. As he approaches his 31st birthday, it's reasonable to think that last season was the start of what will likely be a gradual decline for Swanson in the back nine of his career. This fear is reflected in his early draft price of 195 (SS21), but that could be an overreaction. The Cubs lineup should still be solid around him, and 160 R+RBI should be on the table. His power/speed combo may not be elite, but getting 20 HR/15 SB in that range could prove very valuable. If you miss out on one of the high-end talents at the position, falling back on Swanson wouldn't be the worst thing that could happen. He might not be a massive target, but he's also far from a fade.

2. **Jeremy Peña, HOU (G: 157 SS):** Month-to-month, it was a bit of a bumpy season for Peña, but in the end, he was still a very valuable fantasy asset. His 15 HR, 78 R, 70 RBI, 20 SB, and .266 batting average were good enough for a finish as the SS13 overall. However, his profile is a bit hard to trust when looking forward. His 5.4% barrel rate puts him in the 24th percentile, and his 7.5-degree launch angle and nearly 50% ground ball rate make it pretty likely that he won't be able to be a reliable source of power. While his batting average is very solid, his 3.8 BB% led to just a .308 OBP, which aligns with his career to this point. The Astros lineup around him is also getting older and is not quite the juggernaut it once was, which could jeopardize his counting stats going forward. He predominantly bats somewhere in the middle/lower part of the order, and that's also unlikely to change in 2025. One thing that you should be able to rely on is his base running ability. His 98th percentile sprint speed should lead him to another 20+ SB season. He's an acceptable option, currently going as the SS20 in early drafts, but he's better suited for a middle infield spot than being the first shortstop you take.

3. **Anthony Volpe, NYY (G: 160 SS):** Volpe didn't take the step forward offensively that many people were expecting in 2024. While he did suit up in 160 games, the 23-year-old managed just 12 HR, 90 R, 60 RBI, 28 SB, and a .243 batting average. This was good enough for a finish as the SS14 overall, but still well short of expectations. His power took a major step back, going from a 9% barrel rate as a rookie down to 3.9%, with his hard-hit rate dropping from 42.7% to 34.9%. At his age, there isn't a ton of long-term concern. He will likely figure things out eventually and then be a 20/20 bat for the Yankees, and his outstanding defense will keep him on the field a lot (he's missed just five games over the past two seasons). That said, looking at his profile and expecting him to take that step forward in 2025 is hard. If he makes his way back to the leadoff spot, there is a good chance that he returns value at his 146 ADP. Still, the Yankees moved him down the order in early July, and he never made it higher than fifth in the lineup down the stretch, usually occupying a spot in the bottom third of the order. He may take that step next season, but I'm not banking on it at such a deep position.

4. **Ha-Seong Kim, FA (G: 121 SS):** Kim is entering free agency following what was a down year for him on the surface in 2024. Tricep/shoulder issues ended his season in mid-August after 121 games. In just over 400 ABs, Kim had 11 HR, 60 R, 47 RBI, 22 SB, and a .233 batting average. A promising sign is that while his barrel rate was unchanged from prior seasons, his hard-hit rate rose considerably from 26.2% to 35.4%. His BB% remained stellar at 12.3%, while his strikeout rate (19.8% to 16.4%) and SwStr% (6% to 5.3%) trended in the right direction. His struggles (specifically in batting average) can be tied to his .261 BABIP. Since coming over from Korea, that number has been .281, and Steamer has it projected at .284 for next season, implying that his average will jump back up into the acceptable range. While his eventual landing spot may change how we view him to some extent, buying back on Kim and punting the SS position isn't such a bad idea, considering his incredibly cheap 281 ADP (SS27)

5. **Jose Caballero, TB (G: 88 SS, 37 3B, 31 2B, 1 DH):** Caballero was a savior in the middle rounds (or perhaps off the waiver wire in shallower leagues) for those who needed speed in 2024. Over 139 games, Caballero chipped in 9 HR, 53 R, 44 RBI, 44 SB, and a .227 batting average. While the rest of his line does leave something to be desired, those steals were incredibly valuable, as only three players in MLB had more (De La Cruz, Ohtani, Turang). Caballero looks like he will function in the same role as 2025 for fantasy managers: someone that you can grab late in your drafts to help with speed for those power-heavy team builds. Caballero isn't being drafted until pick 277 (SS26), and it's hard to make sense of that number, considering he finished as the SS20 in 2024. Part of it comes down to Steamer's conservative playing time projections, which only have Caballero playing 97 games. Considering he played 139 last season and there isn't another viable shortstop option in Tampa, Caballero should be able to play nearly an entire season again and provide excellent value on the basepaths. And he won't be a zero elsewhere. His nine home runs with a 5.1% barrel rate might not be exceptional, but he should be able to come close to double-digit power once again.

6. **Brayan Rocchio, CLE (G: 142 SS):** Rocchio had a pretty impressive rookie campaign for the Guardians. He played in 143 games and contributed 8 HR, 50 R, 36 RBI, 10 SB, and a .206 batting average while playing great defense. While he doesn't have much power, he projects as someone who could be very useful in fantasy. Steamer has him going for 10 HR/13SB/.245 average in 2025, which would be immensely valuable considering where he's been going in drafts (467 ADP, SS40). He'll likely be positioned at the bottom of the Cleveland lineup, but to get an everyday player that will likely provide contributions across the board that late in your drafts could be a massive win. You don't need to draft him as your starting shortstop, but investing in Rocchio for depth makes a lot of sense.

AL/NL Only

1. **Orlando Arcia, ATL (G: 157 SS):** Arcia starts off our NL-only tier as one of the most boring players in the pool. He doesn't do much outside of taking the field every day, which can be valuable to those playing in deep leagues. Arcia plays a very solid shortstop and should be able to play 150+ games again in 2025. While that will predominately occur at the bottom of the lineup, he was sprinkled in throughout the middle of the order as many key Braves players missed time in 2024. He's likely relegated back to the nine-hole on most nights going forward, but he should still be able to chip in 15 HR with decent counting stats and a couple of steals in what should once again be an elite lineup.

2. **Max Schuemann, ATH (G: 93 SS, 27 3B, 10 OF, 9 2B):** Schuemann acted as a Swiss Army knife for the Athletics in 2024 as he played six different positions, but predominantly shortstop. Over 133 games, he had 7 HR, 55 R, 34 RBI, 14 SB, and a .220 batting average. He was a solid pick-up for those playing in deeper leagues, but he doesn't have a defining trait for fantasy purposes. He doesn't have much power or speed, doesn't hit for a great average, and does strike out a touch more than we'd like to see. With youngster Jacob Wilson potentially battling for this role in the spring, Schuemann only makes sense as a depth piece on very deep league squads.

3. **Miguel Rojas, LAD (G: 82 SS, 13 2B, 11 3B, 1 1B):** Rojas was a lot more productive than you were likely expecting him to be coming into the season. Over 103 games spent mostly at short, "Miggy Ro" chipped in 6 HR, 41 R, 36 RBI, 8 SB, and an excellent .283 average. The problem with investing a lot into him next season is that the Dodgers will likely find a younger, more suitable option for the future this offseason. Whether that means bringing in a free agent or moving some of their existing parts around, it's hard to see Rojas occupying an everyday role in 2025. He's a decent depth piece in case of injury, but that's about it.

4. **JP Crawford, SEA (G: 104 SS, 1 DH):** After a true breakout campaign in 2023, the bottom fell out from under Crawford this season. He missed time due to hand and oblique injuries, which may be the root cause of his struggles, but whatever the reason, he was a disaster in 2024. Over 105 games, he added just 9 HR, 55 R, 37 RBI, 5 SB, and a miserable .202 average. His strikeout rate jumped by about 3%, and he also lost more than 3% on his walk rate. The most startling drop may be his wRC+ going from a robust 136 down to an 89 mark that is well below the league average. Considering how hard it is to be a hitter in Seattle's home pitcher haven and the relatively weak lineup around him, Crawford is best left for very deep leagues in 2024.

5. **Javier Baez, DET (G: 80 SS):** The fall-off in his production over the last several seasons has genuinely been staggering to watch. Granted, Baez did deal with injuries to his hip, neck, back, and spine in 2024, but it's hard to think his production would have been much better had he taken the field all season. In 80 games, Baez put up just 6 HR, 25 R, 37 RBI, 8 SB, and a putrid .184 batting average. There isn't any hope for a turnaround at this career stage, either. His 43 wRC+ in 2024 suggests that he wasn't even equivalent to half of an average big leaguer, and that's just about all you need to hear to be out on the soon-to-be 32-year-old.

Chapter 10

Outfielders

	OF1	RPV
1	Aaron Judge	18%
2	Juan Soto	15%
3	Mookie Betts	10%
4	Kyle Tucker	10%
5	Yordan Alvarez	-4%
6	Ronald Acuna	-5%
7	Fernando Tatis Jr.	-5%
8	Corbin Carroll	-6%
9	Jackson Chourio	-6%
10	Jarren Duran	-9%
11	Julio Rodriguez	-9%
12	Jackson Merrill	-9%

	OF2	RPV
13	Anthony Santander	8%
14	Jazz Chisholm	8%
15	Kyle Schwarber	4%
16	Teoscar Hernandez	3%
17	James Wood	3%
18	Randy Arozarena	0%
19	Wyatt Langford	-1%
20	Bryan Reynolds	-3%
21	Brent Rooker	-4%
22	Luis Robert	-4%
23	Jurickosn Profar	-6%
24	Mike Trout	-6%

	OF3	RPV
25	Brenton Doyle	4%
26	Spencer Steer	3%
27	Adolis Garcia	2%
28	Brandon Nimmo	1%
29	Cody Bellinger	1%
30	Riley Greene	0%
31	Steven Kwan	-1%
32	Ian Happ	-1%
33	Seiya Suzuki	-1%
34	Michael Harris	-2%
35	Nick Castellanos	-2%
36	Lourdes Gurriel	-4%

	OF4	RPV
37	Lawrence Butler	13%
38	Christian Yelich	12%
39	George Springer	12%
40	Alec Burleson	12%
41	Pete Crow Armstrong	1%
42	J.J. Bleday	-1%
43	Joc Pederson	-4%
44	Dylan Crewes	-5%
45	Lane Thomas	-7%
46	Tyler O'Neill	-9%
47	Jorge Soler	-12%
48	Colton Cowser	-12%

	OF5	RPV
49	Cedric Mullins	5%
50	Kerry Carpenter	5%
51	Josh Lowe	3%
52	Heliot Ramos	3%
53	Parker Meadows	0%
54	Jung Hoo- Lee	0%
55	Roman Anthony	0%
56	Jordan Walker	-2%
57	Byron Buxton	-2%
58	Victor Robles	-3%
59	Lars Nootbaar	-3%
60	Nolan Jones	-5%

***Get updated RPV Cheat for one time $5 cost (free updates)
PayPal: FantasyBlackBook@gmail.com or Venmo: @FantasyBlackBook
And include your email address***

Outfielder/DH Player Profiles and Overview
by Kelly Kirby

Outfielders might seem abundant in fantasy baseball, especially in leagues requiring five in the starting lineup. However, many fantasy managers underestimate how significant the production drop-off is from elite outfielders to the solid ones.

According to the FantasyPros Player Rater, 11 of the top 20 finishers in 2024 were outfielders or designated hitters. Shohei Ohtani's unbelievable 50/50 season put to rest the notion that a DH "clogs" your UTIL slot, and Aaron Judge and Juan Soto turned in superstar performances in New York.

An elite OF1 and OF2 in five-outfielder leagues is a key strategy for fantasy success. This approach provides flexibility at the position while locking in two potential five-category contributors. A solid foundation at outfield allows managers to take calculated risks on rookies like Dylan Crews or players looking to rebound in 2025, such as Michael Harris II.

While there are always waiver-wire gems who turn into league winners, many outfielders end up as replacement-level players who won't move the needle for your team. Finding the right value combo for your rosters is how. Here's how the outfield landscape shapes up for 2024.

The Elite

1. **Shohei Ohtani, LAD (G: 159 DH):** There were a few rumblings about Shohei Ohtani being "overrated" when he was deemed unable to pitch in 2024, but he muted that crowd in a hurry. The 30-year-old fantasy giant turned in an absurd year for managers who let him "clog" their UTIL space on rosters. Ohtani invented the 50/50 club, scored 134 runs, knocked in 130, and slashed a ridiculous .311/.391/1.039. His ISO was a mind-bending .336 on his way to providing 9.1 WAR. Ohtani solidified a terrifying top of the Dodgers lineup and brought home his first World Series ring. He should be ready to return to pitching in 2025, providing an unnecessary bonus from the guy who is already the number-one overall fantasy player. Short of an unforeseen injury, there is no downside to drafting Ohtani 1.1. He will return value in spades. ***AUTHOR'S NOTE *Ohtani as a complete DH/SP breaks the RPV wheel because he's two players in one. He also breaks the RPV scale as a DH only because there are so few of those players at this point in the game's evolution***

2. **Juan Soto, NYM (G: 151 OF, 5 DH):** Regardless of where Juan Soto signs what will inevitably be a monster deal, in 2024, he continued showing why he is also a fantasy monster. First off, he turned just 26 years old at the end of last season, and he remained durable, playing in 157 games. Soto continued doing what he does best: Getting on base (at a .419 clip) while hitting for average (.288). He tacked on a career-high 41 home runs and 128 runs scored while knocking in 109 and stealing seven bags. Where he lands in free agency will affect his counting stats nominally, but if you play in an OBP league, he should be the first guy off the board.

3. **Aaron Judge, NYY (G: 117 OF, 41 DH):** In 2024, Aaron Judge bounced back from a down year (by his standards) to the hitting giant fantasy managers know and love. He led MLB in homers (58) and RBIs (144) and slashed an incredible .322/.458/.701. He cut down on strikeouts, stayed healthy for 704 plate appearances, scored 122 runs, and threw in 10 stolen bases for good measure. Judge benefited from Juan Soto's presence in the lineup, but whether Soto returns or not shouldn't affect what fantasy managers get from him. Judge's age (32) and durability are the only real concerns, but the Yankees have shown a willingness to balance his defense with DHing to keep him in the lineup regularly. He led the league in WAR at 11.2 and will lock down four of the five offensive categories in standard 5x5 leagues. He should be one of the first three players off the board.

4. **Ronald Acuña, Jr. (G: 48 OF):** Ronald Acuña only played in 48 games in 2024 before tearing his ACL and missing the rest of the season, sinking many a fantasy team. As of November, he is not guaranteed to be ready for Opening Day, and we are back in 2023 territory with the superstar. Fantasy managers who took a chance on him after his first knee injury were rewarded with one of the greatest fantasy seasons ever. Acuna hit 41 homers, scored 149 runs, knocked in 106, and stole a whopping 73 bases. Will he do the same in 2025? There is risk, but there aren't many players who profile like the 27-year-old. He should come with a small discount on draft day but keep an eye on his recovery news to ensure he won't miss more than a month.

5. **Corbin Carroll, ARI (G: 156 OF):** Corbin Carroll became the latest Rookie of the Year to struggle with a sophomore slump, though he salvaged his final numbers with an improved second half. Unfortunately for fantasy managers, he failed to live up to his first-round ADP. He still hit 22 homers (11 in August), scored more runs than his rookie season (121 vs. 116), and came within two RBI of matching 2023. His slash line is where things dived, dropping to .231/.322/.428 from .285/.362/.506. His stolen bases also decreased from 54 to 35, even though he played in more games in 2024. Carroll's potential for five-category prowess will keep him high on draft boards, and chances are extremely high that his final line will fall somewhere between his first two seasons. It just might be more comfortable for managers to make him their second pick instead of their first.

6. **Kyle Tucker, CHC (G: 70 OF, 8 DH):** Perhaps no one was more frustrating to roster in 2024 than Kyle Tucker, mostly due to a lack of injury information than the injury itself. It limited him to 78 games, but when he played, he remained the player fantasy managers are used to rostering. He finished with 23 home runs and 11 stolen bases, chipping in 56 runs and 49 RBIs while slashing .289/.408/.585. The 27-year-old showed durability in 2022 and 2023 and will remain a first-round pick in 2025. If there is an injury discount, jump all over it. Tucker is in a contract year and Wrigley should be kind to him.

7. **Yordan Alvarez, HOU (G: 94 DH, 53 OF):** Unlike his teammate, Yordan Alvarez played the most games of any year in his career at 147. He smacked 35 home runs, scored 88 runs, knocked in 86, and even stole six bases (career-high). Alvarez finished with a slash line of .308/.392/.567 and was in the Top 7 in all of baseball in each statistical category. His BB% decreased from 13.9 to 10.9, but his K% also decreased, suggesting he remained discerning with pitch selection. Alvarez will always leave the stolen base column low to empty, but he will provide a steady boost to the other four and should be a first/second-round pick again in 2025.

8. **Fernando Tatis Jr., SD (G: 96 OF, 4 DH):** Fernando Tatis Jr. struggled with some injuries in 2024, but he maintained a high production level when healthy. He appeared in 102 games, hit 21 home runs, scored 64, contributed 49 RBI, and stole 11 bases. His Statcast numbers continue to be stellar across the board. He is in the 99th percentile in hard-hit% and the 97th percentile in average exit velocity and expected batting average. Tatis's days of stealing 25+ bases may be behind him, but he offers excellent ratios and plenty of pop to compensate for it. Depending on what the Padres do in free agency, his counting stats should also see an uptick, with some improvement in those around him.

Top Talent

1. **Julio Rodriguez, SEA (G: 131 OF, 10 DH):** Julio Rodriguez's monthly splits are quite the sight to behold. From April to October, his batting averages went .256, .274, .206, .375, .234, .328. Essentially, if you can find someone willing to trade him back and forth to you monthly, that would be ideal. J-Rod is still only 23 years old and has five-category talent that can't be ignored. He only hit 20 home runs, a far cry from the 32 the year before. His runs and RBIs also decreased significantly to 76 and 68. Perhaps most disappointing to fantasy managers, his stolen bases dropped from 37 to 24. He struggled to be more discerning in pitch selection, carrying a 25.4 K% and a minuscule 6.2 BB% to accompany a ghastly chase percentage of 37.4. Encouragingly, his slash line remained similar to 2023 at .273/.325/.409. Rodriguez will probably be one of the more polarizing players on draft day, but his talent potential is too good to let slip too far. He can still hold down OF1 numbers; just be prepared for some yo-yoing during the season.

2. **Jarren Duran, BOS (G: 160 OF):** Jarren Duran arrived in a big way in 2024 and handsomely rewarded fantasy managers who drafted him. In 160 games played, Duran scored 111 runs, stole 34 bases, hit 21 home runs, and drove in 75. On top of that, he slashed .285/.342/.492, effectively becoming one of the high-end five-category guys that warrant an early-round pick. He can go through bouts of chasing more pitches than he should and sits middle-of-the-pack in Whiff% and K%. His batting average was also slightly higher than expected; however, he projects for another 20/30 season and should kick in another 100 runs, making him an extremely valuable OF2, especially in five-outfielder leagues.

3. **Jackson Chourio, MIL (G: 146 OF, 2 DH):** Welcome to The Show, Jackson Chourio! The highly-touted prospect arrived with a whimper, struggling to get his footing in April and May and leading many fantasy managers to toss him back onto waivers. Those who held on or scooped him up reaped the benefits for the rest of the year. The 20-year-old hit 21 homers and stole 22 bases while slashing .275/.327/.464, which everyone hoped he would do following his incredible stint in Double-A in 2023. Chourio threw in 80 runs and 79 RBIs in a Brewers lineup that sometimes struggled to produce much offense. His Chase% and BB% could use improvement, though they are common struggles for rookies who arrive so young. Fantasy managers should expect a small boost in homers and stolen bases, somewhere in the 25/25 range, as he gets more comfortable with major league pitching.

4. **Jackson Merrill, SD (155 OF):** Jackson Merrill arrived in a big way for the Padres in 2024. The 21-year-old leaped from Double-A to the majors and never looked back. Merrill hit 24 home runs, scored 77 runs, knocked in 90, and stole 16 bases while slashing .292/.326/.500. None of these numbers is a mirage. He is in the 98th percentile in xBA at .308, 96th percentile on xSLG at .547, and 94th percentile in xwOBA at .376. Merrill seems allergic to taking a walk (BB% of 4.9) and chased more pitches than ideal, but that's a trade worth making for fantasy managers. His 2025 numbers should look very similar to 2024, making him a stellar OF2 that you shouldn't be afraid to reach for in the third round of 2025 drafts.

5. **Jazz Chisholm, NYY (G: 97 OF, 45 3B, 4 DH, 3 2B):** Jazz Chisholm gave fantasy managers what they've been looking for since he came into the league: Health. The 26-year-old played in 147 games between Miami and New York, serving as a positional Swiss army knife and getting third base eligibility along the way. Chisholm hit 24 home runs and stole 40 bases while scoring 74 runs and knocking in 73. His counting stats should bounce in 2025, assuming the Yankees improve the lineup around him. Chisholm's Statcast page is still pretty ugly; he sits in the middle or lower in every statistical measure. His slash line of .256/.324/.436 might be the best a fantasy manager can expect, but you're not drafting him for batting average. Take him for the short porch in right field and the 82nd percentile sprint speed, and then just hope he stays healthy.

6. **Teoscar Hernández, LAD (G: 154 OF):** Teoscar Hernández made the most of his contract year. The 32-year-old signed on with the Dodgers and provided the right-handed bat they needed to balance out the monster three at the top of the order. Hernández hit 33 home runs, knocked in 99, scored 84, and stole 12 bases. He slashed .272/.339/.501, continuing to crush against left-handed pitching with a .290 batting average. He also continued striking out at a high rate (K% of 28.8), but his power helps make up for that to some extent. Hernández's fantasy value will be somewhat tied to where he lands. If he returns to the Dodgers or lands in another ideal hitting environment, he will make an excellent OF3 for teams now that's he's right back hitting behind arguably the best 1-2-3 in baseball.

Solid Options

1. **Brent Rooker, ATH (G: 131 DH, 14 OF):** Brent Rooker was a wildly helpful fantasy player in 2024. He hit 39 bombs and drove in 112, scoring 82 runs and stealing 11 bases while slashing an absurd .293/.365/.562. The downside for the 30-year-old is that his .293 batting average is an illusion going forward and should regress to near his career average of .243 next season. The power is real (xSLG of .570), and he was in the 97th percentile in Barrel % (16.6). His 28.8 K% was actually an improvement, which is not promising going forward, as 30-year-olds don't typically improve to this degree. In 2025, the Athletics will play half of their games at Sutter Health Park in Sacramento, which projects to be a hitter's park and could further boost Rooker's counting stats. He will only have DH eligibility in most formats to begin the year, but the list of 40-homer guys is pretty small and might be worth the spot.

2. **Michael Harris II, ATL (G: 110 OF):** Injuries sapped much of Michael Harris's 2024 season, and his stats seemed affected when he was on the field. The 23-year-old also dealt with some bad luck. His slash line was .264/.304/.418, but his xBA was .288, and xSLG was .470. He did reach double digits in home runs (16) and stolen bases (10), which is promising heading into 2025 if he stays healthy. However, each of his first two years has seen fewer games than fantasy managers would like from a draft pick in the fourth round. Harris is a solid option, but it comes with the caveat that he will likely miss time, so he may not be the safest OF2 on the board.

3. **Brandon Nimmo, NYM (G: 147 OF, 4 DH):** Brandon Nimmo had settled into his role as a solid option in fantasy baseball before having a mixed-bag performance in 2024. Of particular note, his always-reliable batting average cratered down to .224 following two years of finishing at .274. His xBA was higher (.247), but that isn't what fantasy managers are looking for with the 31-year-old. What he did provide, though, was another 23 home runs, and he upped his stolen bases from three to 15, a pleasant surprise for those who hung with him. He also added 90 RBI and 88 runs, offsetting his career-low (by a lot) .327 OBP. On this note, his xwOBACON was .390, suggesting we saw an aberration in performance in 2024, and Nimmo should return to a more solid OF3/OF4 option in 2025.

4. **Bryan Reynolds, PIT (G: 133 OF, 23 DH):** Perhaps one of the most reliable fantasy baseball players, Bryan Reynolds continued his consistency in 2024. He hit 24 home runs, knocked in 88, scored 73 runs, and stole 10 bases. He also raised his batting average to .275 from two years of .260s. Reynolds is like that honor roll student in high school who just shows up, does well on his tests, and goes home without ever seeming affected by any of it. There is nothing flashy about the 29-year-old, but we don't need our OF3s to be flashy as much as we want a stable floor. It doesn't get any more stable than Reynolds.

5. **Seiya Suzuki, CHC (G: 72 OF, 59 DH):** Seiya Suzuki dealt with some injuries in 2024 that interrupted an otherwise stellar campaign. The 30-year-old hit 21 home runs, scored 74 runs, drove in 73, and stole 16 bases. He boosted fantasy ratios with an impressive .283/.366/.482 slash line. The only smudge on his stats is a jump in K% from 22.3 to 27.4. Otherwise, his HardHit% and wOBA improved for the third consecutive year, suggesting another solid option to add to outfield rosters in the mid-rounds as an OF3.

6. **Riley Greene, DET (G: 106 OF, 31 DH):** One of the pundits' favorite sleepers last year, Riley Greene delivered an impressive season. The 23-year-old hit 24 homers, scored 82 runs, and drove in 74. While his batting average didn't return to his lofty .288 from the year before, his slash line remained well above average at .267/.347/.457. Greene improved his K% for the third straight year and raised his BB% from 8.4 to 11.0. There is nothing overtly exciting about Greene, which means you should be able to nab him later than the value he will return. If Greene is your OF4, you're in great shape at the position.

7. **Spencer Steer, CIN (G: 102 OF, 63 1B, 7 2B, 6 DH, 1 SS):** Spencer Steer remained a versatile fantasy option in 2024, but fantasy managers suffered from a steep drop in his batting average from .271 to .225. However, the 26-year-old popped 20 home runs and stole 25 bases, 10 more than the year before. The good news is that Steer will still play 81 games in Cincinnati, which will keep his power numbers afloat, and he will bat in a good lineup to keep his counting numbers high. His batting average should be corrected, but the days of .270 are probably behind him, and fantasy managers should expect more in the range of .240. His positional versatility will always boost his draft value but don't overpay for him.

8. **Kyle Schwarber, PHI (G: 144 DH, 5 OF):** Stop me if you've heard this one before. Kyle Schwarber swatted 38 home runs, scored 110 runs, and drove in 104. No player's m.o. remains as consistent as the 31-year-old's, and in 2024, he even kicked in a .248 batting average and stole five bases. He also struck out fewer than 200 times for the first season since 2021, when he only played in 113 games. While age catches up to everyone, 31 isn't that old in a player with his profile, and he will continue batting in a Philly lineup capable of scoring in bunches. On top of that, Schwarber will be a free agent after 2025, meaning we are lined up for a contract-year performance. Protect your batting average somewhere else and reap the power benefits here.

9. **Marcell Ozuna, ATL (G: 162 DH):** Marcell Ozuna returned to the Braves lineup in 2024 and essentially replicated his 2023 performance. He hit 39 home runs, drove in 104, and scored 96. Unlike his contemporary Schwarber, he also hit .302, providing four-category boosts to everyone who drafted him. The batting average is an aberration, inflated due to an unsustainable BABIP of .359, so chances are good he'll regress closer to his career average of .272. Either way, if Atlanta can get itself healthy, Ozuna enters a contract year as a player perfectly worth "clogging" your utility spot.

10. **Jurickson Profar, FA (G: 148 OF, 8 DH, 2 1B):** In 2024, Jurickson Profar set new career highs in home runs (24), runs (94), RBI (85), and batting average (.280). He tied his career high in stolen bases with 10. Currently, he is still a free agent, but no matter where he lands, it will be important to temper expectations for the 31-year-old. Twenty homers are still on the table, but the batting average will drop back to the .250s, and the counting stats will be lineup-dependent. Draft him as nothing more than an OF4.

11. **Adolis Garcia, TEX (G: 131 OF, 23 DH):** After a tremendous 2023 season, Adolis Garcia struggled to meet those lofty expectations in 2024. His home runs dropped from 39 to 25, and his runs and RBIs reduced dramatically, partially due to Texas injuries. What should fantasy managers expect in 2025? Projections have him around 30/75/90, which would be solid OF3 numbers. As of now, his 39/108/107 season looks like the outlier instead of what we should expect.

12. **Steven Kwan, CLE (G: 114 OF, 7 DH):** Injuries took some of Steven Kwan's 2024 season, limiting him to only 122 games, but he made the most of the games he played. His home run total surged to 14, and he still scored 83 runs batting at the top of an impressive Guardians lineup. If you're drafting the 27-year-old, you're hoping for the exact slash line he had at .292/.368/.425. Kwan isn't flashy, but he doesn't strike out or chase bad pitches and is the definition of a "professional hitter."

13. **Ian Happ, CHC (G: 144 OF, 8 DH):** Ian Happ appears to have found his groove as a fantasy player. He'll give you 20+ homers and double-digit steals while taking an abundance of walks, which lead to 90 runs. His K% took a concerning leap in 2024, but the Cubs' lineup is strong enough to warrant an OF3 position on fantasy rosters.

14. **Nick Castellanos, PHI (G: 157 OF, 5 DH):** Nick Castellanos was 100% droppable in May last year. The first two months of the year were atrocious and took his batting average down to more Schwarber-esque depths than what we were used to from Castellanos. It was especially surprising because the 32-year-old tends to get off to a great start. However, he recovered, and the rest of the season played out more like the guy we drafted. Castellanos is still an OF3/OF4 and will have value in that Philly lineup; fantasy managers need just to hope that he reverts to his starts of years past.

Red Flags

1. **Anthony Santander, TOR (G: 130 OF, 25 DH, 1 1B):** Anthony Santander had himself one hell of a contract year in 2024. He set new career highs in games played (155), home runs (44), RBIs (102), and runs (91). He slashed .235/.308/.506 and reduced his K% from 23.2 to 19.4. Santander is now 30 years old, and where he lands in free agency will play a large role in his fantasy value in 2025 and beyond. Assuming he does not re-sign with Baltimore, he is linked to some friendly ballparks (Philadelphia, Washington) for his switch-hitting power. Santander is the rare player with plenty of power without many strikeouts (K% of 20.0). The question is whether his consistency will continue after landing in Toronto. He is a safer mid-round pick than anything early, as some regression is likely in store.

2. **Luis Robert Jr., CWS (G: 97 OF, 3 DH):** Alas, the "Luis Robert has arrived" party in 2024 ended very quickly and in dumpster fire fashion. After a stellar 2023 in which he played 145 games and set massive career highs in all categories, Robert returned to his 2022 self, submarining many fantasy teams that used a second-round pick on him. He played 100 games, but his home runs dropped from 38 to 14. He managed to steal 23 bases, but that was not enough to offset the hellacious .224/.278/.379 slash line. Even more frightening, his xBA was even lower at .215. Sure, Robert was playing on perhaps the most awful team in baseball history, but unfortunately for fantasy squads, he remains in Chicago surrounded by a dilettantish lineup destined for disaster. Without a massive draft day discount, stay away.

3. **Randy Arozarena, SEA (G: 147 OF, 7 DH):** It is difficult to remember a less impressive 20/20 season than Randy Arozarena's last year. His already-high K% (23.9) went up to 26.1, and the off-setting BB% dropped to 11.3. Additionally, his Barrel % dropped from 12.3 to 8.3. This resulted in a slash line of .219/.332/.388. His counting stats also suffered - he only scored 77 runs and knocked in 60. Perhaps the worst news for fantasy managers is that he now plays in Seattle, which features one of the worst lineups and ballparks for any hitter. Do not let Arozarena's name lead you to over-drafting a player who may be, at best, an OF3 but probably closer to an OF4.

4. **Christian Yelich, MIL (G: 48 OF, 26 DH):** Before his nagging back injury reappeared, Christian Yelich was having a renaissance year. He hit 11 homers and stole 21 bases in 73 games, scoring 44 runs and knocking in 42. More impressively, his slash line was .315/.406/.504. This was the Yelich of yesteryear. But the stat to focus on with him is the 73 games. After two years of playing over 140 games, he played the fewest games of his entire career (save for the 2020 shortened season). Fantasy managers will want to keep an eye on any injury news coming out of Milwaukee as we head into 2025, but even then. A 32-year-old Yelich has a giant red flag, so if you draft him, ensure you have a long-term backup plan.

5. **Cody Bellinger, NYY (G: 94 OF, 24 DH, 22 1B):** As expected, Cody Bellinger's stats regressed in 2024 after an MVP-caliber season in 2023. The 29-year-old hit 18 home runs, drove in 78, scored 72, and stole nine bases. He slashed .266/.325/.426 while missing 32 games due to injury. With the somewhat pedestrian numbers, he exercised his player option and will remain on the North Side for another year, though a midseason trade is always on the table, too. The danger with Bellinger is that he repeats his performances from 2021 and 2022 when he was well below average. If you draft him as an OF3/OF4, that seems to be the right expectation, but the red flag of potentially not even reaching replacement-level player status still exists. The move to Yankee Stadium for half his games is about as much as you could ask for in terms of a power rebound.

6. **Mike Trout, LAA (G: 24 OF, 5 DH):** Mike Trout is officially deeply entrenched in the "If only..." category of fantasy (and real) baseball. He started 2024 on an absolute tear and looked like the Trout of old. In only 29 games, he hit 10 home runs and stole six bases. But then that was it. A knee issue kept him out for the rest of the year, leaving fantasy managers who took a flier on him in the late middle rounds wondering what could have been. And now, Trout has every red flag attached to him, with the question of when the right time to draft him in 2025 might be. Before you do, remember that he has not had 500 plate appearances in a season since 2019. Yes, the production you get from him when he is healthy is probably better than 60% of the league, but in head-to-head leagues, that's not going to get you far if he only plays in half the games (or fewer). There is a "right price" for Trout, but the realistic market will make that a double-digit round for the first time in his career.

7. **Nolan Jones, COL (G: 69 OF, 7 DH):** Ouch. Heading into 2024, Nolan Jones had a ton of hype and momentum, which led to him being an early-round draft pick. That was the height of his production, however. Due to injury, he only appeared in 79 games for Colorado, managing a paltry three home runs and five stolen bases after his 20/20 rookie season. His slash line dropped from .297/.389/.542 to .227/.321/.320, and he chipped in only 28 runs and 28 RBIs. Short of Luis Robert, Nolan Jones was the biggest bust of 2024. So now what? It is probably safe to assume we will get stats that land in between those two lines and can hope for 15/15, but don't draft him based on his 2023 production, or disappointment could be in store.

8. **George Springer, TOR (G: 124 OF, 20 DH):** George Springer's red flag is that many fantasy managers still think of him as the player he was with the Astros instead of the 35-year-old with the declining abilities he is now. There is not much upside when looking at his stat profile – his home runs, runs, RBIs, and batting average all declined for the third straight year in 2024. His average, in particular, fell off a cliff to .220, which was by far the lowest of his career. His offensive WAR fell into the negative as well. Springer is, at best, an OF5, and it would probably serve fantasy managers better to draft a player with more upside.

9. **Byron Buxton, MIN (G: 94 OF, 6 DH):** At this point, fantasy managers know the Byron Buxton Rule: Draft him for the talent and with the full expectation that he will be in your IL slot plenty. In 2024, Buxton crossed 100 games for the first time since 2017, making it 102. He hit 18 home runs and slashed a highly respectable .279/.335/.524. His walk rate was minuscule at 5.2%, but his K rate dropped to 25.5% from 31.4% the year before. Those are the positives. He is a risky OF4 or OF5 and shouldn't be drafted before the 20th round in standard leagues.

Serviceable

1. **Joc Pederson, TEX (G 132 DH):** The fulltime move to DH worked well for Joc Pederson, slashing .275/.393/.515 in 2024. That OBP was the best of his career and the SLG% was 4th best. He moves from one strong lineup to another after signing with the Rangers and should be a source of 20+ homers 60 runs and RBI.

2. **Josh Lowe, TB (G: 93 OF, 8 DH):** Josh Lowe was among the more disappointing fantasy players in 2024, mainly because his expectations were so high. He only appeared in 106 games after an injury in Spring Training, and it seemed he could never get going. The biggest fall was in batting average, from .292 to .241. There isn't much to get excited about, but he will steal plenty of bases when healthy. (He had 25 last season.) As long as that's what you're aiming for, Lowe is a serviceable OF4.

3. **Tyler O'Neill, BAL (G: 95 OF, 18 DH):** Tyler O'Neill comes with one very specific tradeoff: He has 30-homer potential, but he will strike out. A lot. In 113 games for the Red Sox in 2024, O'Neill hit 31 homers, drove in 61, scored 74, and slashed .241/.336/.511. Those numbers harkened back to his stellar 2021 campaign. Landing in Baltimore should server him well.

4. **Taylor Ward, LAA (G: 141 OF, 15 DH):** Taylor Ward is good for 25 home runs in 2025 if he stays healthy, and he can provide some solid counting stats, depending on how many games he gets to bat next to Mike Trout in the season. The trick with Ward is that he will tear it up offensively for a month. (March/April: 7 HR, 19 R, 23 RBI, .273 BA – coincidentally, guess which month of the season Trout was healthy…) Then he will fall off a cliff. And then bounce back. If you're prepared to ride out the lows and jump on the highs, Ward can slot in as an OF4.

5. **Garrett Mitchell, MIL (G: 60 OF, 7 DH):** Garrett Mitchell appeared in 69 games for the Brewers and provided promising numbers. He hit eight home runs and stole 11 bases. He also walked at an impressive 11.2% clip and slashed .255/.342/.469. Mitchell slots in as the Brewers' starting center fielder, batting behind Jackson Chourio and William Contreras, which should boost his counting stats. He is an OF5 with some OF4 upside.

6. **Alec Burleson, STL (G: 75 OF, 60 DH, 15 1B):** Alec Burleson came five plate appearances short of 600 and rewarded fantasy managers who grabbed him off waivers, though he faded quickly in September. Burleson doesn't strike out (12.8 K%) but doesn't walk, either. Depending on how the crowded Cardinals outfield shakes out, Burleson could hit around 20 homers in 2025, but he doesn't offer much in the way of upside.

7. **Wilyer Abreu, BOS (G: 130 OF, 1 DH):** Wilyer Abreu saw plenty of action in the Boston outfield and slashed .253/.322/.459 along the way. He sits in the 94th percentile of Hard-Hit% at 50.5, but there is nothing else particularly intriguing about the 25-year-old for fantasy managers. He can competently fill an OF5 slot, but not much more.

8. **Jung Hoo Lee, SF (G: 37 OF):** Jung Hoo Lee played in only 37 games before a torn labrum took the rest of his season. If he remains healthy, fantasy managers can expect a high batting average and a boost to the runs category.

9. **Daulton Varsho, TOR (G: 136 OF, 1 DH):** Daulton Varsho lost his catcher eligibility in 2024, and along with it went most of his fantasy value. His Statcast page suggests he wins the award for "worst hitter who is still serviceable in fantasy." He hit 18 home runs and stole 10 bases last season and is projected for 25/15 in 2025. It's just up to you if you want to take on that anchor to your batting average.

10. **Brandon Marsh, PHI (G: 133 OF):** Brandon Marsh bats in a loaded Phillies lineup capable of scoring runs in bunches. He hit 16 home runs and stole 19 bases in 135 games. He is a strikeout machine (K% 32.4), but his slash line was a tolerable .249/.328/.419. He can be an OF5.

11. **Brendan Donovan, STL (G: 105 OF, 53 2B, 9 3B, 6 DH):** Brendan Donovan is another multi-position fantasy asset who basically isn't going to hurt your team. He hit 14 home runs and stole five bases while slashing .278/.354/.413 in an underperforming Cardinals lineup. St. Louis will plug and play him wherever they need him, which is what fantasy managers can do, too.

12. **TJ Friedl, CIN (G: 83 OF, 2 DH):** TJ Friedl wasn't really healthy until August 2024, which zapped his value for fantasy managers who drafted him hoping for a 20/20 season. Chances are high that his 2025 numbers will land somewhere between 2023 and 2024, but we can never rule out the boost playing in Cincinnati can give.

13. **Parker Meadows, DET (G: 82 OF):** Parker Meadows is the projected leadoff hitter for a frisky Tigers lineup. In 82 games, the 25-year-old hit nine home runs and stole nine bases. He tore up Triple-A pitching when he was there, so there is plenty of upside to taking a flier on Meadows as an OF4.

14. **Victor Robles, SEA (G: 87 OF, 2 DH):** There is an argument to be made that Victor Robles won some managers their leagues in 2024. He batted .389 with 13 stolen bases in the season's last month. His .307 average is definitely a mirage (xBA .261), but the speed is real when he gets on base. He should remain affordable in drafts, making him a decent OF4/OF5.

Up and Coming

1. **James Wood, WSH (G: 79 OF):** James Wood got the July call-up and played 79 games for the Nationals in 2024. His showing was a mixed bag, though he gradually improved in August and September. Wood hit nine dingers and stole 14 bases. He scored 43 runs and drove in 41 while slashing .264/.354/.427, and he is slated to be a daily fixture in Washington's lineup next year with solid 20/20 potential. Wood will be among the more highly sought-after "young guys" in the draft, driving up his price. However, the allure of his stats in Triple-A last season will make the Rookie of the Year candidate worth the gamble in the fifth round or so.

2. **Wyatt Langford, TEX (G: 109 OF, 25 DH):** Wyatt Langford was THE guy coming out of Spring Training in 2024, and he had a very up-and-down season in his rookie year. It ended in exciting, promising fashion when he batted .300 in September, hitting eight of his 16 home runs with 20 RBI and 25 runs scored in the month. Langford looks like the type of player who suffered "freshman difficulties" but may miss the "sophomore slump." Fantasy managers can hope for a 20/20 season (he went 16/19 in 2024), and he should see an improvement in counting stats if the Texas lineup around him stays healthy. He is a perfectly solid OF2/OF3 with plenty of upside for a fantasy team.

3. **Lawrence Butler, OAK (G: 123 OF):** Lawrence Butler arrived in 2024 and promptly hit 22 home runs while stealing 18 bases and providing a boon to all fantasy managers who picked him up off waivers. The 24-year-old played in 125 games, drove in 57, scored 63 runs, and slashed .262/.317/.490. These numbers were in line with his expected stats. How the change in ballpark for the Athletics will impact the hitters remains to be seen, but there is talent in that lineup to be had. Butler is a decent mid-round draft pick with 20/20 potential, slotting in as an OF3.

4. **Brenton Doyle, COL (G: 146 OF, 3 DH):** Brenton Doyle made vast improvements in his second year in the league. He reduced his K% from 35 to 25.4 and raised his BB% from 5.1 to 7.6. He batted a respectable .260, though his .317 OBP left something to be desired. His real value lies in his counting stats. The 26-year-old hit 23 home runs and stole 30 bases in an ugly Rockies lineup. He scored 82 runs and drove in 72, providing plenty of fantasy value for those who rostered him. If Doyle's numbers stay steady, he is a solid OF3 with OF2 potential.

5. **Dylan Crews, WAS (G: 31 OF):** Dylan Crews got his first cup of coffee in the majors and took off running. Literally. The 22-year-old stole 12 bases in 31 games while hitting three home runs and slashing .218/.288/.353. If you're drafting Crews, you're looking for his speed to get you in the range of 25 steals with some possible power upside. Don't expect his slash numbers to improve significantly, but they should get within a range to not do damage. As with all the names in this group, don't overpay for what you'll probably get. Somewhere in the 13th round or beyond seems about right for an OF5.

6. **Evan Carter, TEX (G: 41 OF, 4 DH):** Evan Carter took the world by storm when he arrived in 2023 for the Rangers and went bonkers in 23 games. However, injuries ate up his 2024 season, leaving him healthy for only 45 games and 162 plate appearances. Essentially, the 22-year-old is having a do-over year in 2025, and fantasy managers can still hope for a 15/15 season with solid counting stats for their OF5 roster spot.

7. **Heliot Ramos, SF (G: 112 OF, 8 DH):** Heliot Ramos had a nice rookie season for the Giants, hitting 22 home runs and driving in 72, with a perfectly acceptable slash line of .269/.322/.469. The good news for fantasy managers is that these numbers align with his expected stats, giving us a reasonable projection for 2025. When it comes time to fill your OF5 spot later in the draft, Ramos provides a pretty stable floor for a guy entering his second full MLB season.

8. **Heston Kjerstad, BAL (G: 19 OF, 13 DH):** Heston Kjerstad has had two short stints in the majors, and his second one offers some upside for the future. Kjerstad has hit for average at every level of the minors, and with a longer stay in Baltimore, chances are good he will offer a good slash line, as his OBP has also been solid in his career. With the potential departure of Anthony Santander to free agency, Kjerstad slots in as the Orioles' starting right fielder. The at-bats should be there, and he is worth a flier as the last pick in your draft.

9. **Pete Crow-Armstrong, CHC (G: 117 OF):** Vaunted prospect Pete Crow-Armstrong got his first extended look in Chicago, and he responded in kind with 10 home runs and 27 stolen bases. While he only hit .237, his track record in the minors suggests this should improve in his second full season. He'll never be an on-base machine (xwOBA .281), and his Statcast page is as blue as his uniform. But he offers enough upside, particularly with his 99th-percentile speed, to slot in as an OF3 on most rosters.

10. **Colton Cowser, BAL (G: 146 OF, 1 DH):** Colton Cowser's rookie season proved to have a little more pop than expected but was otherwise in line with what analysts anticipated. Cowser hit 24 home runs and stole nine bases while slashing .242/.321/.447. He had a high K rate (30.7%) and didn't walk much (9.3%), but he's batting in a good Baltimore lineup, so his counting stats could see a boost from last year's 77 runs and 69 RBIs. The 24-year-old has plenty of room for growth and should be a fantasy asset in 2025.

11. **Jasson Dominguez, NYY (G: 16 OF, 1 DH):** While it feels like we've been talking about Jasson Dominguez for years, he is still only 21 years old and has destroyed Triple-A pitching every time he lands there. Dominguez can potentially be a perennial 20/20 guy, giving him plenty of fantasy value worth drafting in 2025. The Yankees should have room for him in a lineup that vastly underperformed in 2024, and the upside might be too intriguing to pass up. Just temper expectations for the typical struggles that befall most rookies.

12. **Roman Anthony, BOS (Rookie):** There is a strong argument for Roman Anthony to be considered a Top 5 prospect in baseball, and there is a good chance he will land in the majors sooner rather than later. Anthony's plate discipline greatly improved from Double-A to Triple-A last season, and across the two levels, he hit 18 home runs, stole 21 bases, and slashed .291/.396/.498. In terms of upside and depending on the size of your roster, Anthony is definitely worth a stash if you have the room.

AL/NL Only

1. **Lourdes Gurriel Jr., ARI (G: 127 OF, 4 DH, 1 1B):** Lourdes Gurriel Jr. offers fantasy managers a stable floor to build around, particularly in NL-only leagues. He'll hit around 20 home runs and bat in the .275 range. The Diamondbacks lineup offers plenty of opportunities for counting stats as well.

2. **Ceddanne Rafaela, BOS (G: 87 OF, 82 SS, 10 2B, 4 3B):** Ceddanne Rafaela offers a little bit of everything and has positional flexibility to boot. Expect stats in the 15/20 range, but don't expect him to get on base at a decent clip (.274 OBP in 2024). He is fine in AL-only leagues and debatable in mixed leagues.

3. **Jorge Soler, LAA (G: 46 OF):** Jorge Soler signed a three-year deal with the Angels in the offseason, where he will continue doing what he does: Hitting between 20-30 home runs and going 75/75 in the other counting stats.

4. **Kerry Carpenter, DET (G: 47 OF, 35 DH):** Kerry Carpenter gets on base at a healthy clip (xwOBA of .379) and should get managers close to 20 home runs. The Detroit lineup has plenty of potential, making the 27-year-old a late-round option to round out your outfield spots.

5. **Cedric Mullins, BAL (G: 140 OF, 1 DH):** Cedric Mullins had a bounce-back year in 2024 regarding his speed, raising his stolen base count to 32 from 19 and playing 147 games. He still has a little pop in his bat, hitting 18 home runs, which aligns with his 2025 projections. The Orioles' lineup is crowded, but he is an acceptable option in AL-only leagues.

6. **Lars Nootbaar, STL (G: 107 OF):** Lars Nootbaar dealt with more injuries in 2024 but continued to get on base and hit the ball hard. If he can stay healthy, he could produce a 20/10 year and have enough upside to draft as your final outfielder in NL-only leagues.

7. **Lane Thomas, CLE (G: 51 OF, 1 DH):** While the power from 2023 didn't carry over, Lane Thomas made up for it with his legs (32 SB) and still hit 15 home runs. He is projected to bat in the middle of a decent Cleveland lineup and has the upside to go 20/25, making him worth strong consideration in AL-only and deeper mixed leagues.

8. **JJ Bleday, ATH (G: 157 OF, 1 DH):** JJ Bleday quietly turned in a solid year for Oakland, hitting 20 home runs and lowering his K% by four points. He will never hit for average, but depending on how the ballpark in Sacramento plays, a 20/75/75 year is well within reach.

9. **Jake McCarthy, ARI (G: 137 OF, 1 DH):** Jake McCarthy is gonna do what Jake McCarthy always does. He will steal between 25-30 bases, pop a few home runs, and provide a decent batting average. He makes for a nice fifth outfielder in NL-only leagues.

10. **Jacob Young, WAS (G: 149 OF, 1 DH):** Jacob Young seemingly came out of nowhere to steal 33 bases in 2024. His slash line of .256/.316/.331 isn't going to hurt your roster from the fifth outfielder spot. However, if you want to wait on stolen bases, Young will be available late in drafts and provide that need.

11. **Jo Adell, LAA (G: 123 OF, 5 DH):** Now, there was the season many were hoping for from the prospect who had been previously so disappointing. Adell went 20/15 with 54 runs and 62 RBIs and demonstrated good bat speed and barrel percentage. If you believe the upside might still be there, he can be a flier in AL-only leagues.

12. **Jesús Sánchez, MIA (G: 119 OF, 19 DH):** It's easy to overlook Jesús Sánchez because it's easy to overlook the entire Marlins team. But don't be fooled. Sánchez offers good power with a solid batting average and should hit double digits in both homers and steals. He is a sneaky good pickup in NL-only leagues.

Chapter 11

2025 Prospects

By Chris Welsh

It's prospect time for the 2025 Fantasy Black Book! This year, we're doing things a little differently. The following ranks will be more hyper-focused on the 2025 fantasy baseball season. The top 25 is a mixture of my top prospect list, with variations weighted to prospects who will produce this year. You won't find prospects in this first portion that won't play in the bigs.

There is also some distinction between players that can have more production versus half a year when weighing how good they are. Let me give you an example. Kristan Campbell, for the Red Sox, is a no-brainer top-15 prospect in baseball for dynasty. I believe he is more talented than quite a few players listed ahead of him, but there is no guarantee he will break camp with the team or even up within the first few months.

So, a few prospects rank above him here due to getting more at-bats. Even his teammate, Marcelo Mayer, seems a bit more likely to get a shot in the majors before Campbell, but in Dynasty, I would easily take Campbell over Mayer.

These top 25 prospects would be my focus in 2025 redraft leagues, either to draft or stash. I also have a few highly ranked dart-throw names and five top-10 prospects who are talented but far away.

Top 25 Prospects

1. **Jasson Dominguez, NYY, OF:** Dominguez goes into 2025 as my top prospect overall if we are looking at 2025 only. If Soto doesn't return to New York, all the production is open for Dominguez. If Soto returns, he should still see significant at-bats. Dominguez is still prospect-eligible after just 56 at-bats in 2024. His stats weren't big, but he put up an above-average barrel percentage at 10.6% and an over 45% hard-hit rate. His strikeout rate was too high in the majors at 28%, but he did sport an 18% strikeout percentage at Triple-A in 2024. Early Steamer projections have him at 141 games, putting up a 20/20 season.

2. **Dylan Crews, WAS, OF:** Crews, like Dominguez, is still prospect-eligible going into the 2025 season. Between Double-A, Triple-A, and the majors, Crews hit 16 home runs and stole 37 bases. Crews hit just .212 but had an xBA of .256 with a solid 44.7% hard hit percentage. He had an 89% zone contact percentage in Triple-A and an 87% zone contact percentage in the majors. His strikeout rate of under 20% at the majors gives an excellent baseline for his hit tool moving forward. He hit a majority of his at-bats out of the leadoff spot. If that continues with his bat and stolen base potential, Crews could push to be a 20/30, high-run player this coming year. We have Steamer projections, which show him at 17 home runs and 24 stolen bases in just under 140 games played.

3. **Andrew Painter, PHI, SP:** Painter had not pitched in the minors since 2022 due to injury. He was able to join up in the Arizona Fall League, where I was able to see four of his six starts. Painter returned to his original form, touching 99 on his fastball and throwing a strikeout-inducing slider in addition to his other offerings. He pitched just 15 innings but won the AFL's pitcher of the year. He commanded, walking just four batters to his 18 strikeouts, and did this all despite giving up some hard contact. Painter looks the part of the number one pitcher in the minors. His problem will be pitching 15 total innings since 2022. The Phillies are already talking about him joining the rotation this season. You would imagine he is capped at around 100 innings, and Steamer has him right at 102. Betting on pitching prospects, in general, is risky, but Painter's stuff is there, and he's one I'd bet on later in drafts for redraft leagues

4. **Jackson Jobe, DET, SP:** Jobe struck out 96 in 91.2 innings with a 2.36 ERA in the minors. He had a small cup of coffee in the majors with two appearances where he struck out two, giving up no hits in four innings. He touches 97mph but sits 94-95mph with his fastballs and offers a four-pitch mix. FanGraphs Stuff+ system did rate all four of his pitches 120 or higher Stuff+, which makes them above-average pitches. If Jobe starts generating more swings on his stuff, which could happen with major league catchers helping him become less predictable, he could have a big rookie year. Steamer projects out 140+ innings pitched with pretty mediocre stats. I'd say he can beat expectations. He ranks this high due to him going right into the rotation. He'd be outside the top nine or ten if this were an overall dynasty without proximity.

5. **Matt Shaw, CHC, 2B:** Shaw is on a rocket ship of prospect value going into the 2025 season. He finished the year hitting .284 with 21 home runs and 31 stolen bases. Shaw struck out less than 20% of the time at Double-A and Triple-A. Once the year finished, he played with Team USA in the Premier 12 tournament. He destroyed that league, making the all-world team and leading in most offensive categories. Shaw keeps his hands inside and explodes on the baseball, showing off contact ability and real power projection. He's currently blocked in Chicago, but trade rumors could open up an everyday spot for him to break camp with the team. Steamer projections don't see him with a ton of at-bats, but if you pushed the numbers out to around 150 games, Shaw would put up an almost 25/25 season. He's an early Rookie of the Year top candidate.

6. **Jordan Lawlar, ARI, SS** Lawlar had a rough 2024. He missed most of the first part of the year with a torn ligament in his thumb, followed by a lingering hamstring injury. It was nearly a lost year. He was having a hot spring training, to which he could add a .367 average with two home runs in 12 Triple-A games. Due to missed time, he played in the Dominican Winter League, hitting exceptionally well and showing off some above-average power potential. He is a real power/speed combo threat. In 2023, he hit 20 home runs and stole almost 40 bases. Consistency is a problem, as he still has a strikeout problem he needs to clean up. The other is just staying healthy. The Dbacks love Perdomo and have Marte at 2B. There could be an opening in center field, in which one scenario could be Marte moving back to CF, or another is the Dbacks seeing Lawlar like the Padres did with Jackson Merrill and giving him a shot in the outfield. He could rocket up draft boards if this happens and is announced early.

7. **Coby Mayo, BAL, 3B:** Mayo had a solid 2024 minor league season. He hit .296 with 25 home runs in just over 350 at-bats. He had a small stint in the majors that did not go well. He had four hits in 17 games with an over 40% strikeout percentage and a 24% hard hit rate. There was almost nothing to take out of his major league time. His confidence must have been shot, as he struggled in his last

few minor league stints of the year. He's shown to be an over-average power hitter, consistently putting up 110 exit velocities in Triple-A and solid barreling numbers. His strikeouts are a problem; he is not just counting the major league number, but he struck out around 25% of the time in Triple-A. The Orioles have done a good job working with their minor leaguers once they get to the majors. Mayo is only projected on Steamer for 30ish games, but over a 150-game span would project for 25 home runs on Steamer, who usually is pessimistic about rookie performances.

8. **Roman Anthony, BOS, OF:** It's hard to find a prospect who had more helium in 2024 than Roman Anthony. He played at Double-A and Triple-A when he was just 20 years old. He finished with 18 home runs, 21 stolen bases, and a .291 average. Most of his power came at Double-A, but once he moved up to Triple-A, he hit over .340 and cut his strikeout rate under 20%. He's showing a consistent ability to make contact, supporting this as he had an over 86% zone contact percentage while also getting on base. He had an over .400 OBP in 2023 and followed up this past year at just under .400. He posted a 90th percentile exit velocity (108) at Triple-A, which shows his ability to not just step into a lot of contact but quality hard-hit contact. I believe there could be some questions on how big the homerun and stolen bases totals look at the majors after those declined when he went up to Triple-A, but that is a short-lived idea and tracks more to this year. Long term, the sky is the limit. Anything is still young, which could make the Red Sox continue slow-rolling him, but his time in Triple-A is a great sign that he has an impact this season. If we hear the Red Sox will let him compete out of camp or he is traded to a destination where he starts immediately, he will rocket up redraft boards.

9. **Kumar Rocker, SP, TEX:** Kumar Rocker's early career has looked like a roller coaster: The ups of being drafted, the downs of getting hurt and missing a year, further downs of horrible production, and then a rocket up with his 2024 production. He struck out 55, with a 1.96 ERA in 10 minor league starts. He carried over his great year to the majors, with a 3.86 ERA, an xERA of 3.17, and a 25% strikeout percentage over three starts. The keys to this bounce back and why you can buy into it are twofold. He could throw his fastball with velocity for strikes, something he hadn't done before. The second, most likely setup by his fastball, was the dominance of his slider. It has a deep plane with a 50% Whiff rate in the majors. This will be the reason why he could put up big strikeout numbers. He's expected to join the rotation in 2025. Steamer has him at 134 innings, an over-nine K/9, and a 3.80 ERA. Most prospect people wrestle with the long-term value, but with what we are seeing now, he's a great bet in the prospect world for at least this upcoming season.

10. **Jacob Wilson, SS, ATH:** It took just a little over 300 at-bats after being drafted for Jacob Wilson to get called up to the majors. He's a high-contact, low-strikeout hitter in the mold of Luis Arraez. In the minors in 2024, he had a .433 batting average across two levels while striking out just 15 times in over 200 at-bats. He's never showed off great power, but he had seven home runs in both of those stops in the minors. The environments were hitter-friendly, but it showed off some slight power potential. Once called up, he hit .250 and struck out just 9% of the time in his short stint before an injury. We could get more excited if he stole any bases of impact, but he's currently a much better points league player than anything else. He'll be the starting shortstop for the Athletics this year, which might give him a leg up on other rookies from a pure production standpoint.

11. **Rhett Lowder, SP, CIN:** Lowder started 22 games in the minors with a 3.64 ERA and a 1.11 WHIP. He pitched 30 innings in the majors, picking up two wins and putting up a 1.17 ERA. He throws a lot of strikes but held hitters to just a 3.3% barrel rate. Being in the rotation all season is a huge plus; the ballpark is not. Luckily, with his command comes lower flyball rates. He gave up just nine home runs in a bit over 100 innings pitched. He's a low velo pitcher but has a decent shot to put up quality starts.

12. **Chase DeLauter, OF, CLE:** Had he stayed healthy, DeLauter could have been up in the majors during the 2024 season. He has struggled with injuries over the last two-plus years. He hit eight home runs in under 40 games during the minor league season. He finished the year in the Arizona Fall League, playing limited games but still hitting .340 with double the walks and strikeouts. He has a short follow-through swing, similar to Mike Trout. He has plus power and a low strikeout rate. He doesn't chase outside of the zone. If he stays healthy, he could possibly break camp with the team. Worst case, we should see him early in the year.

13. **Marcelo Mayer, SS, BOS:** Mayer played 77 games at Triple-A, hitting .307 with eight home runs and stealing 13 bases. There seemed to be an approach change, as he hit more groundballs, which isn't great, but his line drive percentage jumped from 15% to 26%. This approach change also equaled a career-low strikeout percentage of under 20% at the highest level of the minors. Mayer may end up in a Dansby Swanson-like role when given an opportunity. He's currently blocked with the Red Sox, but they could make a fix soon or a trade. The trade option would make Mayer an even better 2025 option, but likely a more limited power/speed guy.

14. **Colson Montgomery, SS, CHW:** Montgomery put up his first minor league season of over 100 games, a positive after an injured 2023. The negative was with his 18 home runs, and he hit just .214 at Triple-A. It was his worst contact-based season, but there were rumors he had continued injury issues during the year. He played in the Arizona Fall League for the first half, where he showed an advanced eye, pitch selection, and a massively lower strikeout rate. There is a path for him to break camp with the big league team. Projections have him getting a lot of playing time, but nothing in the data supports a good average for them. His AFL is encouraging, and if he carries that over, He could put up a 20/10 rookie campaign.

15. **Kristian Campbell, SS, BOS:** Campbell was the most significant breakout prospect of 2024, winning Baseball America's Minor League Player of the Year award. He completed three levels in the minors, hitting .330 with 20 home runs and stealing 24 bases. Campbell played SS, 2B, and CF in 2024, which provides versatility and a path to early playing time. His hit tool looks legit. While posting an 88% zone contact rate, he barrels the ball at a high clip and posted some solid hard-hit numbers. Projections favor his average while giving minimal counting stats, but if given an entire season, I could envision a Jackson Chourio-like year for Campbell. When he will get the call up is what leaves some of this as a question.

16. **Carson Williams, SS, TB:** Carson Williams had a big breakout year in 2024, hitting 20 home runs and stealing 33 bases in Double-A, where he spent the entire season. He's a defensive wizard, but the offense is still coming along. He hit just .256 and had a 28% K rate and a 64% zone contact rate. The latter two are more concerning than anything. He spent time after the season refining his skills with Team USA in the Premier 12 tournament. The Rays have slow-rolled prospects, but he has a good relationship with Junior Caminero, is major-league glove-ready, and has a bat that can work in the majors. Due to the slow roll, we may not see him until mid-year. If he comes up early, I could see him statistically playing out like Spencer Steer, with impactful home runs, stolen bases, and a struggling average.

17. **Thomas Saggese, SS, STL:** Saggese spent most of the season in Triple-A, hitting .253 with 20 home runs. Once seen as more of a contact hitter, he was able to turn that into impactful power. He had a small callup to the majors before the year ended and spent the offseason in the Arizona Fall League. His approach looks to be low strikeouts and doubles contact. He sacrificed some average for power during the year but went back to an average-based approach in the AFL. Projections have him near half a season of at-bats but spread out over an entire season, he would come close to a 20/10 season with a .240 average.

18. **Owen Caissie, OF, CHC:** Caissie posted a big Triple-A at just 22 years old, hitting .278 with 19 home runs and 11 stolen bases. Known more as a power hitter who posts some immense exit velocities and has some stereotypical strikeout issues, striking out 28% of the time in Triple-A this past year. Caissie was added to the 40-man roster which means he can easily be added to the roster anytime. Caissie could get a shot if the Cubs either move some major league bats or involve him in a trade to another team. If given the chance to play most of the year, he could put up 25-plus home runs.

19. **Braxton Ashcraft, SP, PIT:** Braxton Ashcraft may be the next in line of big Pirates pitchers. Ashcraft dominated Double-A with a 10.59 K/9 and a 3.69 ERA in 53.2 innings. He followed that up in Triple-A in 19 innings, posting a 0.47 ERA and a sub-two BB/9. He offers a mid-90s fastball, a plus curveball, and a changeup. Pirates Bubba Chandler has a higher ceiling and made it to Triple-A, but Ashcraft is already on the 40-man roster, so we will most likely see him before Chandler.

20. **Brandon Sproat, SP, NYM:** Sproat pitched 116 innings in 2024, striking out 131 batters with a 3.40 ERA. Sproat hits triple digits with a plus fastball while getting whiffs on his changeup and slider. He got hit a bit once he moved up to Triple-A, but he should be a big strikeout option as a fantasy pitcher. Some spots in the Mets rotation could allow him to start. Projections have him up to 83 innings this year in 15 starts with a 4.16 ERA.

21. **Drake Baldwin, C, ATL:** Baldwin hit .276 with 16 home runs in just under 500 at-bats. He spent the off-season first playing in the Arizona Fall League and then moving over to play with Team USA's Premier 12 league. Travis D'Arnaud's leaving opens up a legitimate opportunity to break camp with the big league team.

22. **Caleb Durbin, 2B, NYY:** Durbin may be just 5'6, but he packs a punch. He hit 10 home runs in 2024 while stealing 31 bases. He then went to a second straight AFL, hitting five more home runs and breaking the AFL record for stolen bases at 29. The Yankees have already mentioned him as an option as a starter at second base. Projections on an entire season see him over 10 home runs and 30 stolen bases. He's a late hidden gem.

23. **Deyvison De Los Santos, 1B, MIA:** De Los Santos has been an odd traveling man, going from the Dbacks to the Guardians, back to the Dbacks, and then traded to the Marlins. De Los Santos has 90 career home runs but at just age 21. He hit 40 home runs this past season.

24. **Agustin Ramirez, C, MIA:** Agustin was the centerpiece of the Jazz Chisholm trade. He finished the year with a .267 average, 25 home runs, and a surprising 22 stolen bases. He posts elite hard hit, barreling, and 90th percentile exit velocities. A full-season projection from Steamer puts him over 20 home runs and 10 stolen bases as a catcher in an entire season, but he is currently only around 60 games. The bigger questions are his actual playing time and when the Marlins pull the trigger.

25. **Quinn Mathews, SP, STL:** Mathews did the "Jackson Holliday" but pitched at and moved up all four levels of the Cardinals system. He won Cardinals MiLB Pitcher of the Year, throwing 143 1/3 innings, striking out 202 batters with a sub-one WHIP, and putting up a 2.76 ERA. He's already 24, so the Cards have put him on the fast track to the majors. Steamer projections have him at 83 innings pitched in the majors. If he breaks camp with the team, he could push 160 in the majors.

Five More To Watch

1. Ronny Mauricio, SS, NYM
2. Moises Ballesteros, C/1B, CHC
3. Christian Moore, 2B, LDouble-A
4. Kyle Teel, C, BOS
5. James Traintos, 2B, CHC

"So you're saying there's a chance?" Prospects

1. **Travis Bazzana, 2B, CLE:** The 2024 number-one overall pick has shown off massive power, contact, and on-base skills. He spent the off-season playing in Australia. It's highly unlikely he will get major at-bats in his first full year with the team.
2. **Bryce Eldridge, 1B, SF:** Eldridge played at all four levels in 2024, but this was his first full season after being a two-way player. He spent some time in the AFL but left halfway through to avoid burnout. He is being drafted high in NFBC early, with some guessing he could be up early like Jackson Holliday, but I think the Giants play it slower, with him starting at Double-A.
3. **Samuel Basallo, C, BAL:** Basallo is a top prospect who, like many Orioles prospects, is just blocked. He shows off above-average bat-to-ball skills and legit power potential. He is stuck to playing either catcher or first base, both blocked at the major league level. A trade could open up more potential time, but I'd speculate his impact comes late into the 2025 season.
4. **Spencer Jones, 1B, NYY:** Jones spent the 2024 season at Double-A. He's a player with whom we use the "freak" tag. Standing 6'7, he hit .256 with 17 home runs and 25 stolen bases. He struggled with his average early in the year and has a massive hole in his swing. He struck out 36% of the time. If he were to get a call, he's the type you gamble on due to his skill set, but he'll likely be slow-rolled until he fixes those strikeouts.
5. **Jac Caglianone, 1B, KC:** The two-way player spent all of 2024 after being drafted this year as a hitter. He put up some ugly swings and overall lackluster production until he played in the 2024 Arizona Fall League. He became more selective, tapped into his power, and, as he told me one day, one of his home runs registered over 500 feet. He wants to break camp with the Royals, but the team will likely want to see him more consistent before they bring him up. This isn't even tapping into the potential pitching side, which could delay things.

Top 5 Fantasy Prospects Not Listed Due To ETA

1. Walker Jenkins, OF, MIN
2. Max Clark, OF, DET
3. Sebastian Walcott, SS, TEX
4. Leo DeVries, SS, SD
5. Lazaro Montes, OF, SEA

Made in United States
Orlando, FL
19 February 2025